Teaching To Transform

Perspectives on
Mennonite Higher Education

Keith Graber Miller, Editor

PpP
Pinchpenny Press
Goshen, Indiana

Theron Schlabach's "Goshen College and Its Church Relations: History and Reflections" reprinted by permission, with some adaptations, from Richard T. Hughes and William B. Adrian, eds., *Models for Christian Higher Education: Strategies for Success in the Twenty-First Century* (Grand Rapids: William B. Eerdmans, 1997).

Cover art by Bruce Bishop, "The Adelphian Fountain" ©1994.
Used by permission.

Cover and book design by Erin Clymer.

PpP
Pinchpenny Press
Goshen College
1700 S. Main St.
Goshen, IN 46526
Tel: 219.535.7450
pinchpennypress@goshen.edu
Fax: 219.535.7293

Pinchpenny Press is a project in chapbook publication begun in 1969 by Nick C. Lindsay and sponsored by the English Department of Goshen College.

To our students,
who give us hope
for the future of the church
and the world

TABLE OF CONTENTS

FOREWORD

Although Mennonite voices were once absent or marginalized in discussions about church-related higher education, over the last decade they have been welcomed by our Catholic and Protestant colleagues. Several of the essays in this volume had their genesis in conferences or publications associated with the Models for Christian Higher Education project, a Lilly Endowment-funded study which included Mennonite perspectives alongside Catholic, Reformed, Lutheran, Evangelical/Interdenominational, Wesleyan/Holiness, and Baptist and Restorationist ones. Other chapters were stimulated by the Rhodes Consultation on the Future of the Church-Related College, with which I have been associated since its inception in 1995. In an upcoming discussion panel at a Harvard University conference on The Future of Religious Colleges, four religious traditions will be represented: Roman Catholic, Reformed, Evangelical, and Anabaptist.[1] More than ever before, Mennonites are having opportunities to articulate and disseminate their vision and mission for higher education.

Since at least the 1960s, Mennonite educators have hoped for a coherent, constructive philosophy or theology of higher education. While some essays here offer brief, systematic treatments, we do not purport to provide a thorough-going Mennonite theology or philosophy. Some of us involved in recent on-campus and ecumenical conversations will continue to reflect on these themes in the new century, working toward more systematic presentations in the future. In this volume, we hope to join a thoughtful, zesty chorus of others who have addressed issues regarding Mennonite higher education in conferences, institutional histories, and edited texts written by those from many traditions.[2]

Distinctive about this contribution to the ongoing conversation is that all of the essays, with the exception of the closing chapter, were written by active Goshen College faculty and administrators. Chapter One, which is adapted from my presentation at the national Models for Christian Higher Education conference at the University of Notre Dame, presents an overview of a Mennonite model for higher education. Chapter Two, written by Professor of History Theron F. Schlabach, is an insightful analysis of Goshen College's history and its relationship with the Mennonite Church. The third chapter is President Shirley Hershey Showalter's search for an "Anabaptist Voice," a voice which would allow us to "return again to the world with something to give and something to say." Chapter Four, by Academic Dean Paul A. Keim, comes out of Goshen's recent general education materials and puts forth a vision for the liberal arts. Goshen College's Study-Service Term (SST) is discussed in a number of the essays, but is most clearly given a philosophical and theological foundation in the fifth chapter, written by Director of International Education Wilbur J. Birky. In Chapter Six, Associate Professor of Education Kathy Meyer Reimer and recent graduate Scott Barge model and discuss collaborative learning.

Among the most provocative chapters in this volume are those which deal, either implicitly or explicitly, with "dissociation," the drifting away of colleges and universities from the vision and structures of their founding denominations. Of those Christian colleges founded before the Civil War, about 80 percent had ceased to exist by 1930, a legacy which haunted advocates for church colleges during the last century. Over the past 30 years, more than 100 church-related colleges have been shut down or have separated from their founding denominations. Today about 725 church-sponsored higher education institutions, nearly 200 of them Catholic, continue to function across the American educational landscape.[3]

Providing a backdrop for Theron Schlabach's previously mentioned essay is this dissociation phenomenon. Albert J. Meyer, longtime Executive Secretary and President of the Mennonite Board of Education, picks up the theme directly in Chapter Seven, suggesting how to maintain "lively long-term church-school relationships." In tackling such issues as faculty hiring, board and staff personnel and leadership, and student recruitment, Meyer is wading into waters with many undercurrents. Opinions differ. These are issues actively under discussion on college campuses and in their supporting churches.

At a time when Goshen and other Mennonite colleges in the United States are contemplating, with great intensity, their institutional identity and their relationship with the newly forming Mennonite Church USA, this volume seems particularly appropriate. In the present merger of the Mennonite Church and the General Conference Mennonite Church, one of the complex issues is how the denomination and its colleges will relate.

In any event, I am grateful to many persons for allowing this timely text to come to fruition. Beth Martin Birky, Ervin Beck, and the Pinchpenny Press board have been particularly gracious in encouraging publication of this collection. The Lilly Endowment, through its stimulation of nationwide discussions about church-related higher education, has provided opportunities and collegial support for these reflections. The Rhodes Consultation on the Future of the Church-Related College has piqued my own interest and research on the issues addressed here, and a grant from the Consultation has provided some of the funding for publication. Rebecca Rich, my teaching assistant, did some of the initial copy-editing for the text. Erin Clymer, who recently published her own Pinchpenny Press book, did a yeowoman's job of copyediting the remaining chapters as well as masterfully designing and laying out the entire book. Lyle Miller of Goshen College's Printing Services provided helpful assistance in technical details, paper selection, and actual printing of the text. My family – Ann, Niles, Mia Bei, and Simon – allowed me to spend what could have been a lighter May term at my office collecting data and editing the text. The authors of each essay worked collegially and congenially with me in adapting their writings to this format.

Woven throughout the completed book is the question, What does it mean to remain an Anabaptist-Mennonite college in the 21st century? Although many might answer this question differently, for at least some of us it means valuing the college's Mennonite heritage, rooted in biblical faith and Anabaptist historical understandings. It means creating an environment where all are welcome, and the needs of all who come are served. It means embracing the gifts and intelligences of everyone in the community. It means recognizing Jesus as the fullest expression of God we know, and having a commitment to God, whom we believe to be a God of grace, peace, and justice. It means valuing a continuing relationship between the church and the college. It means striving for academic excellence for the purpose of Christian service, and affirming intellectual curiosity wherever the search for truth may lead. It means believing in the importance of interaction with and sensitivity among persons of different cultures and nations, promoting an international perspective rather than a parochial one. It means having some mutual accountability and support in the college community, and being a companion to the earth and to all of God's creation. It means consciously seeking to liberate ourselves and others from materialism, consumerism, hedonism, and individualism. It means prophetically critiquing our culture, but also participating fully in the best of it and taking seriously our responsibilities as citizens.[4]

All of this suggests that we continue to stand in the tradition which birthed us – a living, breathing tradition which is capable of adaptation and change, and which continues to nourish us from our roots. May we remain committed to being an open, welcoming, inclusive Mennonite college, a community of faith, learning, and transformation for those both beyond and within the Mennonite fold.

Keith Graber Miller
Goshen College

---

1. I am grateful to Albert J. Meyer, former Executive Secretary and President of the Mennonite Board of Education, for calling this Fall 2000 conference to my attention. In personal correspondence, Meyer wrote that "one of the remarkable developments of the past decade has been the inclusion of 'Anabaptists' as a separate category distinguished from 'Roman Catholics,' 'Mainline Protestants,' and 'Evangelical Protestants' in research studies, data analyses, and symposia." Meyer said that in his work in the 1970s and 1980s, "Anabaptists" were classified with other groups in most research studies, but that has changed over the past decade. "It is significant," he said, "that the 'Anabaptists' singled out for special recognition are a far smaller group than those in the other categories and that some much larger denominational groups are lumped in with others in the larger categories. There is no question about the fact that Mennonites are seen as having something significant to contribute in today's discussions."

2. See the bibliography at the end of this volume for recent texts addressing these concerns.

3. Most of these statistics are taken from Stephen Haynes' introductory chapter, titled "Will the Paradox Endure?: American Church-Related Colleges and the Postmodern Opportunity," in Stephen Haynes and Corrie Norman, eds., *Talking Out of Place: Professing in the Postmodern Academy* (Waco: Baylor University Press, forthcoming).

4. Most of this paragraph is drawn from the unpublished conclusions about Goshen College's "core identity" made by a 1996 on-campus faculty discussion group, which I facilitated as part of the Rhodes Consultation on the Future of the Church-Related College. Paul Keim and I made minor adaptations to the list when we presented a 26 February 1999 convocation titled "Choice and Fate: Goshen College and Mennonite Identity in the 21st Century."

1

TRANSFORMATIVE EDUCATION

Keith Graber Miller[1]

Several years ago, at a conference on Mennonite higher education at our sister college in Bluffton, Ohio, Doug Reichenbach, the father of a Mennonite high school student, articulated his image of what he expected a church college to be for his son someday.

"One thing I expect," Reichenbach said, "is inspiration. I expect that if my son goes to a Mennonite school he will be able to breathe in, take a deep breath of, the Holy Spirit; to breathe in a sense of acceptance, to breathe in a sense of the church and the faith. To take a deep breath and feel that he is loved and cared for."

"The second thing I would expect," said the father, "is an opportunity for him to express his imagination." He noted that different language has been used to express such creativity, including the oft-cited, "Do not be conformed, but be transformed by the renewing of our minds." "But it is more than thinking," said the father. "I would like my son to find a place at a Mennonite school where his images could be released. Whatever those images are – verbal, artistic or some other kind of creativity. Someplace where his imagination can let go."

"The third thing I expect," said Reichenbach, "is that he will experience some interrelationship like he has not experienced before. I expect the church school to provide opportunities for community for him. To share himself, to be in a personal relationship with faculty. To be in a relationship with friends, persons from other cultures, and all kinds of interrelationships."

"Fourth," he said, "I expect him to experience identification on two fronts. I know our son needs to leave our household to find himself. I know he has to separate himself from his parental home. I know he needs to find his identity. But more than that I know my son, who has just recently made a commitment to Jesus, needs to understand about whose he is, the Lord to whom he belongs. I expect him to experience that kind of identity but also identification with Christ and Christ's church, particularly the Anabaptist-Mennonite expression of the church."[2]

Reichenbach's image of a Mennonite college encompasses much of our tradition's rich heritage of full-bodied, earnest discipleship; voluntarism; a biblicism which acknowledges the lordship of Christ; pacifism; an ecclesiology of a mutually accountable and covenanted body of believers; a willingness to be countercultural regarding those parts of culture that need to be countered; and a wisdom born out of experience and commitment. Education modeled after such a charge is, or would be, education toward life-giving transformation – transformation of self, community and society. As Goshen College President Shirley Hershey Showalter has said, a Mennonite model for Christian higher education "transforms thinking by living and by one's commitment to a radically Christocentric lifestyle."[3] What this suggests, in pedagogical language, is an emphasis on experiential learning or praxis, an ongoing process of action and reflection which builds on both social analysis and cultural immersion. Such a pedagogy recognizes that education is not value-neutral: it is either liberating or domesticating. It also acknowledges the need for learning to be dialogical, and expresses the hope that education be transformative – of self, community, and society.

Mennonites' Entry into Higher Education

Mennonites were latecomers to the higher education ball, Cinderellas who founded our colleges in the late 19th and early 20th centuries, long after most others had begun the dance. While our Presbyterian and Catholic and Methodist counterparts were doing the minuet, we were out hoeing. When they moved into break-dancing and then moshing, we were still folk dancing. More over, by the time we made it to the ball, many church-related educational institutions had come and gone – closing or leaving behind their denominational partners.

Mennonite efforts at establishing colleges were manifestations of both an *embracing of* and a *resistance to* acculturation.[4] As we, undoubtedly clumsily, waltzed into higher education, we were following the lead of other Protestant and Catholic traditions, simply doing as others had done. *Some* Mennonite colleges were established to keep Mennonite young people from imbibing too deeply in other streams. As has been true for several other religious traditions, it was said that "You could send a Mennonite to Harvard. You just couldn't get one back."[5]

At Goshen College, the founding intent was *not* to safeguard the Mennonite tradition; the college's roots are less sectarian, though even more inauspicious, than that. As we will see in Theron Schlabach's historical essay in this volume, Goshen began in 1894 as the Elkhart Institute, a privately owned *commercial* enterprise, but after a year the fledgling school got the support of a board of Mennonite church leaders. When the institute moved to Goshen in 1903, it changed its name, came under full denominational affiliation, adopted its motto "Culture for Service," and began a long, supportive, and sometimes turbulent relationship with the Mennonite Church. The college's first president, Noah E. Byers, said he wanted early 20th-century Mennonites to avoid the "intellectual· starvation" that comes from rethinking the same thoughts, and he challenged them to open themselves so they could experience "even more the richness and beauty of a large life." Byers knew from his own experience in a university college of arts and sciences that "higher education, if approached from the liberal arts tradition, was understood to be a quest: revelatory, transforming, beneficial."[6]

Such a vision is not always a safe one, and as it was institutionalized in the early decades of Goshen College's history, it led to the one-year closing of the school (which was perceived by the church as too liberal or progressive) in 1923-24. The college reopened in September 1924, though less volatile forms of the essential, dynamic, creative tension between the church and the college have remained. The irony of such a tension – and the lingering ambivalence about Mennonite higher education – is that nearly 80 percent of the Mennonite young people who come to our colleges stay in Mennonite churches throughout their lives, and most *leaders* in the church have been educated in our colleges and seminaries.[7] The figures for "keeping our own" – or participation in any religious body after graduation – are much lower for those Mennonites who go to other colleges.[8]

Today, of course, we educate not only our own daughters and sons, but those of others as well. Similar to some Catholic institutions, about 65 percent of our students come from our own tradition. Some of those diverse Mennonites, or their parents, are sufficiently acculturated that they would not necessarily share Doug Reichenbach's vision of a church-related school. The other 35 percent of our students include those from Catholic, Presbyterian, Methodist, Lutheran, Episcopalian, Baptist, nondenominational, unchurched, Hindu, Muslim, Buddhist, atheist, and agnostic backgrounds.

We pray that for *all* of our students, Goshen's community of faith and learning will develop, as our mission statement and desired outcomes declare: faith that is active and reflective; intercultural openness; the ability to communicate effectively and think actively and strategically; an understanding of the transcendent reality of aesthetic and spiritual experience; personal integrity that fosters the ability to resolve conflict and promote justice; leadership abilities that empower self and others; an understanding of responsible stewardship; a sense of vocational direction; and a healthy understanding of self and others that is reflected in social relationships of interdependence and mutual accountability.

On our campus, we continue the energizing process of seeking to serve our diverse students while remaining faithful to a not-fully-articulated Mennonite educational philosophy. When I hear colleagues at other colleges and universities speak about the "Reformed model for higher education" or the "Catholic intellectual tradition," I confess to feeling a smidgen of theological envy. Not only were we latecomers to the higher education ball, once we finally arrived we came without fully securing our theological or philosophical dancing shoes. Over the last decade, multiple, profound voices have begun to craft an authentic philosophy and theology of Mennonite higher education – one that *sings* (or perhaps *dances*, if we don't want to engage in metaphor mixing). But we are still looking for the theological glass slipper, or maybe simply the moccasin or sandal, that slides on easily.

Before addressing briefly Mennonite higher education and biblicism, incarnationalism, internationalism, integrity and interdependence, a word should be said yet about our Anabaptist ancestors. Some of the key emphases of our 16th-century forebears were the necessity of voluntary baptism rather than infant baptism, based on an adult commitment to follow in the way of Christ; a rejection of violence; and the freedom of the church with respect to the state in matters of worship and religious practices.

In a seminary course for which I was a teaching assistant at Emory University, the professor once read one of the many Anabaptist diatribes against the pope and Rome. Squirming in my seat, conscious of my good Catholic friend sitting next to me, I said, "I'm sorry, Pete. We didn't mean it." And without missing a beat, he said, "That's OK, we got you back." And he was right. While many 16th-century Anabaptists were highly educated, they and others in the fledgling movement were martyred by the thousands in the early years. The loss of such leaders, and the fact that the primary antagonism toward Anabaptists came not from common folk but from other theologians and philosophers, contributed toward a relatively anti-intellectual stream in our tradition's middle centuries.[9]

In many respects, premodern Mennonites foreshadowed dimensions of postmodernism. Some may see this simply as premodernism *dressed up like* postmodernism. Perhaps so. But while Mennonites are far from anti-foundationalist, they have long been suspicious of universal reason. As a people on the margins throughout most of their history, Mennonites accepted early on that no publicly espoused master-narrative was inclusive enough to include them. That made them distrustful of meta-narratives and public rhetoric's potential manipulation, giving them a thoughtfully critical, discerning, and countercultural edge. Mennonites have been content to remain faithful to their history and religious tradition, perceiving themselves as biblical "salt and light" rather than wielders of power over nature or nations. As pacifists who only recently added "justice" to their vocabularies, Mennonites generally have contented themselves with working at local levels and seeking to serve and empower in scattered communities around the world rather than in national power centers.

Their historic commitment to unadulterated honesty, letting "their 'yea' be 'yea' and their 'nay' be 'nay,'" may permit greater openness in seeking after truth – wherever God's truth may be found. As some developmental theorists suggest, "the greater the truth commitment, the more uncertain the commitment to other attitudes and opinions" since such a commitment provides a dynamism leading to potential revision or overthrow. "The ardent truth seeker shakes up comfortable presumptions, including those of the truth seeker herself," say Anne Colby and William Damon in their book *Some Do Care*, though they add that not *all* other beliefs may be up for grabs since a "core commitment of honesty can coexist with other central articles of faith."[10]

Mennonites also have rejected the Enlightenment notion of dismembered individuals, unencumbered selves abstracted from particular formative narratives, commitments, relationships, and communities. At Goshen, in our Bible and Religion department's teaching of Hebrew and Christian Scriptures, we hope to breathe life into the text, or rather to allow the text's hot, moist breath to touch students. The people whose stories are told are real people who have experienced God in genuine ways, and who, in the midst of their many failures, are tremendously devoted to God, knowing God as their Creator and Redeemer and Sustainer.[11] In what we call the Ten Commandments, the first word is not a rule but a call to remembrance of God's mighty acts. Before God tells the Hebrew people not to worship other gods or to make idols, God says, "I am the Lord your God, who brought you out of the land of Egypt." As a response to God's mighty acts, the people were then called to be faithful. Discipleship is not a call to drudgery, but a response to the grace given to us in and through and because of the one we call Christ.

I suspect our Jewish sisters and brothers often live closer to the text than we do. For 30 centuries the descendants of Abraham and Sarah have begun the Passover ritual with the youngest son asking the father, "Why is this night different from all other nights?" And the father says, "We celebrate tonight because we were slaves to Pharaoh in Egypt, and the Lord our God delivered us with a mighty hand." There is a kind of immediacy about the way the account is given, a *placing of oneself* into the story and an *embracing* of the story as one's own. We hope those who call themselves Christians, including many of our students, can weave themselves into these particular narratives, and grant authority to the text which has shaped those who have come before them.

Our 16th-century forebears, fallible as are their descendants, sought to be faithful to God's call to represent – to re-present, as Rod Sawatsky says in his chapter in *Models for Christian Higher Education* – the Word in the midst of the world. "From the Anabaptist perspective," writes Sawatsky, "Jesus as the Word made flesh reveals God's will for His disciples, His church ... so, too, the Mennonite college is to be incarnational."[12] For Mennonites, and for students at Mennonite colleges, such incarnation[13] frequently is expressed in sweaty, tactile, embodied discipleship, often translated into service and peacemaking. Such service can be broadly defined, though, allowing most vocations to be understood as or transformed into loci for Christian service.

Service and Experiential Learning

Richard Hughes, professor of religion at Pepperdine University, noted insightfully that Mennonite understandings of discipleship and community are what sustain the life of the mind in Mennonite contexts. "After all," writes Hughes, "if one builds community around a commitment of service to others, one inevitably respects the other and the other's point of view .... Clearly, the Mennonite commitment to service-oriented community enhances the life of the mind insofar as it enhances serious conversation with a variety of cultures and with perspectives different from their own."[14]

At Goshen, as at many other colleges and universities today, service opportunities – and options for other experiential and cross-cultural education – abound. On our campus several hundred students voluntarily participate in local community service each year – with Habitat for Humanity; with La Casa, which provides assistance to new immigrant families and others; with The Window, an inter-church agency which provides food for those needing it; with Big Brothers/Big Sisters; and with other community and church organi-zations.[15] Each year four students live with two developmentally dis-abled young adults in a college-owned house, in an effort to integrate persons with disabilities into a more mainstream living arrangement. Every summer about a dozen students participate in our Ministry Inquiry Program, which places them in congregations across the country as ministerial interns, and scores of others participate in required practica, internships and other experiential learning.

Where service, experiential learning and cross-cultural education are most clearly institutionalized, however, is in our Study-Service Term (SST). As Theron Schlabach and Wilbur Birky discuss in their essays in this volume, all Goshen students are required to complete SST or a comparable international education requirement. While small and, until relatively recently, limited primarily to European ethnic ancestry,[16] Mennonites – along with their educational institutions and mission organizations – have developed a remarkably international perspective. Such internationalism can be traced, in part, to persecution which frequently forced Mennonites to move from their homelands into strange territories – to the American colonies, Russia, Paraguay, Canada and elsewhere. It also is rooted in the denomination's pacifism. Because members of the church usually seek conscientious-objector status in times of warfare, they have sometimes been referred to as "anti-American." Mennonite ethicist John Richard Burkholder says this response could better be described as "more-than-Americanism." Pacifists, writes Burkholder, "consciously adopt a more global worldview than most Americans. They wear tribal identifications lightly and see themselves as global citizens."[17]

As one early summary of SST stated, to be effective, the study-abroad term must allow students to have vivid, firsthand experiences so they can "punch through what has become for many the confusion, impersonality, and vacuity of life in sterile, suburban America."[18] Such an intention – and the desire to place students where the majority are in the minority racially, socially, linguistically and religiously – necessitates that SST programs be located in developing countries, or places which have been on the receiving end of colonialism. Throughout each academic year Goshen students, accompanied by Goshen faculty members, are in such settings as Dominican Republic, Costa Rica, Côte d'Ivoire, Mali, China, Indonesia, and the former East Germany. On SST students live with and – to the extent possible – become a part of families. During their seven weeks in their capital city they read, engage, reflect and journal on their experiences as well as participate in lectures by artists, intellectuals, educators, and theologians from their host country. For the second half of the semester-long program, they move out into the countryside alone or with one other student (again living with families) and participate in low-key service projects, working alongside their hosts, accompanying them as they harvest their crops or care for their ill, elderly or orphans; teaching and learning; or staffing medical clinics. SSTers recognize that they cannot truly "help" their hosts in a brief, six-week period, and that their main calling is to encourage those in the villages to believe in themselves and to draw on their own faith and other resources, working together as communities to bring about change.

If we can continue to communicate its rootage in our faith commitments, international education programs such as Goshen's Study-Service Term can appropriately school Mennonite and other young people in the virtues and perspectives of their own faith stories while expediting their entry into a postmodern world with appreciation for multiculturalism, knowledge of diverse narratives, and commitment to dialogical humility.[19]

Transforming Faculty

SST undoubtedly transforms our students. But it also transforms – personally, spiritually, intellectually, and pedagogically – the more than half of our faculty who have led SST units. We learn to love our students through the intimacy of living alongside them in a place of disorientation. We learn to be vulnerable as we stumble through learning and relearning second languages. We learn how to teach by observing our hosts.

While I was in Haiti in 1997 with our Dominican Republic SST students, we heard from Father Roger Desir, a Haitian Episcopal priest. His lecture was one of the best presentations I have heard in my life. He had lived through all of Haiti's turbulent history of the last several decades, and he had been jailed because of his advocacy work, and he had spent 17 years translating the Bible into Creole so his people could read the text in their own language. He had been committed to a life of service, and his passion and commitment had given him a kind of character which made him believable, which made us *want* to sit at his feet. I was moved nearly to tears, and humbled when I thought of my own shabby teaching in light of his.

Graduate school catapulted me out into the classroom with vigor, and what I lacked in teaching experience I made up for in rookie's zeal. But after four years of teaching I sensed I was getting stale, and that I needed more outside stimulation. I needed fresh insights from the world beyond the campus. Leading our international education program did that for me – for now, for a time. My hope is that I never forget how needful I am, how needful we all are, of passions and experiences outside the classroom – internships in schools if we teach education; time in churches or with social-service agencies if we teach Bible and religion; engagement in the business world if we teach in that department; the occasional international education experience to reinvigorate our sensibilities. As teachers, we need ongoing experiential learning if we are to have anything to teach. And with such learning, we also will be able to better value such a pedagogy. Experiential learning in international settings – for Goshen's teachers as well as students – renews, restores, matures, provokes, transforms, and educates – toward excellence and toward wholeness.

And just a word more yet about integrity. As Yale's Stephen Carter reminds us, "The word *integrity* comes from the same Latin root as *integer*, and historically has been understood to carry much the same sense, the sense of wholeness: a person of integrity, like a whole number, is a whole person, a person somehow undivided."[20] Though we too often fail, as teachers and administrators at a Mennonite institution, we seek to model and foster such integrity – a wholeness that is concerned not only with intellectual acuity but with honesty, consistency, character formation, spiritual growth, emotional stability, and interrelational sensitivity. At Goshen, "faculty" is a designation given not only to those of us who teach but to administrators and campus counselors and admissions personnel and student development team members and resident dorm directors, a recognition that teaching and learning happens across the campus, in both the visible and the invisible curriculum, the ethos of the place.

In a world peopled by radical individualists living fragmented lives, we want our students to be whole, to recognize the interrelationship of their various dimensions, to make commitments, and to acknowledge their dependence on their Creator, the earth, and their companions on the journey. One way this interdependence is best symbolized on our campus is in our frequent hymn-sings, consistently the best attended chapels of the year. A music ritual performed at times of crisis by the Mbuti, the pygmy hunter/gatherers of Zaire, is the *molimo*. In the *molimo* the singers employ a technique known to musicologists as *hoquet*, in which "the individual notes of any melodic line are ascribed to individual singers, so that no one singer carries the entire melody but each carries an essential part of it and all are therefore equally necessary."[21]

Our four-part singing in chapels, singing of hymns from our own traditions as well as others, embodies this reality: all parts are essential for the blended, rhythmic passion of the hymn, and we *carry* each other into this self-transcending, communitarian moment. The message is not lost on students. And so we sing.

And we continue to search for a theology and philosophy of Mennonite higher education that sings. Through conversations with others who have longer denominational histories in higher education, and through dialogue with faculty and administrators in other Mennonite colleges and universities, we are beginning to craft, from the soles up, our philosophical and theological dancing shoes. We pray that we can remain authentically rooted in our faith tradition, and that we also can humbly learn from others. And we pray that we all may be faithful to our callings as administrators and teachers in this holy, transformative practice of higher education.

---

1. Keith Graber Miller is Professor of Bible, Religion, and Philosophy at Goshen College. This essay is an expanded version of his presentation, titled "Exploring a Mennonite Model at Goshen College," at the Models for Christian Higher Education: Strategies for Success in the 21st Century conference, 12 June 1998, University of Notre Dame. Portions of this essay were part of Graber Miller's contribution to a chapter he co-wrote with Shirley Hershey Showalter titled "Keeping the Faith: Integrity with Your Heritage," in Pamela Schwandt, ed., *Called to Serve: St. Olaf and the Vocation of a Church College* (Northfield: St. Olaf College, 1999).

2. Panel, "The Expectations and Responsibilities of Conferences and Local Congregations vis-à-vis Mennonite Higher Education," in Ken Hawkley, ed., *Mennonite Higher Education: Experience and Vision: A Symposium on Mennonite Higher Education* (Bluffton College, 1992), 137.

3. Richard T. Hughes, "Introduction," in Richard T. Hughes and William B. Adrian, eds., *Models for Christian Higher Education: Strategies for Success in the Twenty-First Century* (Grand Rapids: William B. Eerdmans, 1997), 5-6.

4. See Paton Yoder's "Toward a Mennonite Philosophy of Education Since

1890" (multilithed "Philosophy of Christian Education Study for the Mennonite Church: Workshop Paper C," 13-16 September 1968, Hesston, Kansas), 3. Available in the Mennonite Historical Library (hereafter MHL), Goshen College.

5. Some of our institutions of learning were founded more to provide "guarded education" or "guarded liberal education" than "higher education," as Paul Lacey said about his own Quaker tradition at the Imagination and Reflections for Church-Related Higher Education: Models Meaningful for Mennonites conference, April 1997, Goshen College.

6. Susan Fisher Miller, *Culture for Service: A History of Goshen College, 1894-1994* (Goshen: Goshen College, 1994), 35.

7. In a response to an earlier draft of this essay, Albert J. Meyer, former Executive Secretary and President of the Mennonite Board of Education, wrote, "As an integral part of the Mennonite Church, Goshen College's model has been different: Goshen has been expected to be a vision leader as well as a teacher of young people and future leaders in its denomination .... Whether or not this will continue to be the case, it would seem to me to be an important part of the understanding of the Goshen model in the past century. Goshen is not simply 'under' the denomination. It is not 'equal' to the denomination, whatever that might mean. Goshen has a specific and key leadership role within the denomination; a role on which both church and school depend for their health and mission-accomplishment in the future."

8. Perhaps more surprisingly for some of our constituents, only about 60 percent of those Mennonites who do not go to college at all remain in Mennonite churches. The figures gleaned here are from several studies completed over the last two decades, including: LuEtta Friesen, "College Attendance and Church Involvement, First Mennonite Church, Middlebury, Indiana, 1970-1995" (unpublished report, 1995); Don Garber, "Education and Oak Grove Church," *Gospel Herald* (30 December 1980), 1049; and Brenda Detweiler, et. al., "Study of Lancaster HS Grads Between 1970-1980" (unpublished report).

9. Marlin E. Miller, president of Associated Mennonite Biblical Seminary until his early death, wrote: "The major reason for [Anabaptist and Mennonite] suspicions of the dominant theologies was based on the ways they saw theological interpretation used to detract from the hard sayings of Scripture (for example, in relation to baptism or the rejection of violence), or to justify doctrines which appeared to make no demands (faith apart from discipleship), or to perpetuate a form of legalism by putting all doctrines on the same level. They also decried what seemed to be a lack of careful controls for interpreting the sense of Scriptures and the reservation of theology for the experts only. For them the true test of a theological statement was its compatibility with the life and doctrine of Jesus Christ and the apostles. The measure of true theological understanding depended not primarily upon the level of intellectual ability but upon the openness and abandonment to God's will as revealed in Jesus Christ and the teaching and example of the apostles. Throughout their subsequent history, Mennonites have frequently dogmatized this critique and expanded it into a general anti-theological stance rather than discriminating between good and bad theology." See Miller's "Theology," in Cornelius J. Dyck and Dennis D. Martin, eds., *Mennonite Encyclopedia*, Volume V (Scottdale: Herald Press, 1990), 882. When I headed off to Atlanta for my Ph.D., my own mother, God bless her, said, "Well, OK, but I just hope you don't turn out like some of those weirdos."

10. Anne Colby and William Damon, *Some Do Care: Contemporary Lives of*

Moral Commitment (New York: The Free Press, 1992), 77. As early as 1914, one Mennonite professor at Goshen College, John E. Winters, warned students about being closed to new truths. "The thinking individual, he wrote, not only has the prerogative, but he is under a moral obligation to inquire into his own beliefs .... *Never fear to inquire into the truth! Truth will always bear the closest scrutiny.*" John E. Winters, "Two Dangers in Student Life," *Christian Monitor* (February 1914), 447-448, as cited in Paton Yoder, "Toward a Mennonite Philosophy," 16.

11. In making reference to God as Creator, I should acknowledge the grossly underdeveloped theology of creation among Mennonites. Rodney J. Sawatsky suggests that a stronger emphasis on creation would serve Mennonite higher education well: "A fully developed doctrine of creation is important not only for the areas of culture and the arts but also to enable Mennonites to respond appropriately to nature and the environment and, in turn, to have a more balanced appraisal of history and human activity." See Sawatsky, "What Can the Mennonite Tradition Contribute to Higher Education," in Richard T. Hughes and William B. Adrian, eds., *Models for Christian Higher Education*, 198. Mennonites' fear of creation theology is linked partly with their pacifism, and is mediated from Karl Barth through the influential theological ethicist John Howard Yoder. Part of the fear stems from using creation theology to justify certain unjust orders of creation. In "The Invisible Curriculum – On Being Wisdom's School," in Harry Huebner, ed., *Mennonite Education in A Post-Christian World* (Winnipeg: CMBC Publications, 1998), Thomas R. Yoder Neufeld, makes several significant forays into creation theology, noting, in part, that the biblical writers' "attentiveness to wisdom often took them beyond the confines of their own communities and traditions, believing as they did that God's wisdom informs *all* of creation, and can therefore be encountered profitably in the courts and stoas of other peoples." For some initial efforts at Mennonite creation theology, see, e.g., Calvin W. Redekop, "Toward a Mennonite Theology and Ethic of Creation," *The Mennonite Quarterly Review* 60 (1986), 387-403; Peter C. Erb, "Reflections on Mennonite Theology in Canada, *Journal of Mennonite Studies* 1 (1983), 179-190; and A. James Reimer, "The Nature and Possibility of a Mennonite Theology," *Conrad Grebel Review* 1 (1983), 33-55.

12. Rodney J. Sawatsky, "What Can the Mennonite Tradition," 195. The incarnational motif also is important for valuing the material world: if God comes to us in the flesh, as the Christian tradition has affirmed, one must take seriously earthly matter. Such a perspective provides at least some theological warrant for earth-keeping as well as the arts. On incarnational language, see also Wilbur J. Birky's essay in this volume on Goshen's Study-Service Term.

13. Historically, incarnational language has been underdeveloped among Mennonites, though it seems rich with possibilities. Part of the problem may be that several early Anabaptists, including Menno Simons and Dirk Philips, adopted a "heavenly flesh" teaching regarding Jesus. They misfortunately asserted "that Jesus' humanity (flesh) was nourished in Mary, but that it originated in heaven and did not receive its substance from Mary. They based this position partly on Jn 6 and I Cor 15 and partly on the Aristotelian view that the mother's seed is entirely passive." Such a teaching "may have influenced some Mennonite concepts of church, salvation, and Christian ethics considerably longer [than the mid-18th century], perhaps even until the present. The concept of the pure church, linked originally with the heavenly flesh Christology, has most likely contributed to both perfectionism and

divisions among Anabaptists and Mennonites throughout history." See Marlin E. Miller, "Christology," in Cornelius J. Dyck and Dennis D. Martin, eds., *Mennonite Encyclopedia,* Vol. V, 148.

14. Richard T. Hughes, "How the Lutheran Worldview Can Sustain the Life of the Mind," in *From Mission to Marketplace,* papers and proceedings of the 83rd annual meeting of the Lutheran Educational Conference of North America (Washington, D.C., 1997), 12.

15. In recent years, each fall a Celebrate Service Day has been scheduled to allow faculty, staff, and students to spend the day together doing community service projects.

16. It should be noted, however, that non-Western, non-white Mennonites around the world are now in the majority in Mennonite denominations.

17. John Richard Burkholder, "Pacifist Ethics and Pacifist Politics," in Michael Cromartie, ed., *Peace Betrayed? Essays on Pacifism and Politics* (Washington, D.C.: Ethics and Public Policy Center, 1990), 198.

18. "The Study-Service Trimester Abroad," March 1971, 10. Available in MHL.

19. For a fuller analysis of Goshen's SST program, see my "A One-Armed Embrace of Postmodernity: International Education and Church-Related Colleges," in Stephen R. Haynes and Corrie E. Norman, eds., *Talking Out of Place: Professing in the Postmodern Academy* (Waco: Baylor University Press, forthcoming).

20. Stephen L. Carter, "Becoming People of Integrity," *Christian Century* (13 March 1996), 297.

21. Colin Turnbull, "Liminality: A Synthesis of Subjective and Objective Experience," in Richard Schechner and Willa Appel, eds., *By Means of Performance* (New York: Cambridge University Press, 1990), 81. I am indebted to Tom F. Driver, *Liberating Rites: Understanding the Transformative Power of Ritual* (Boulder: Westview Press, 1998), 152, for this reference.

2

GOSHEN COLLEGE AND ITS CHURCH RELATIONS: HISTORY AND REFLECTIONS

Theron F. Schlabach[1]

To this day, Goshen College has kept "conclusive" marks of "a full-bodied, unapologetic church relationship": governance through church boards; a majority of the faculty being Goshen graduates; all tenured faculty having to be Mennonite "or share the spirit of Mennonites"; a rule that 65 percent of the students be Mennonite; and an ethnic feel about the campus. But rather than having a "fortress mentality," Goshen's people "are open and at ease with a visitor." Neither are they by any "means all of one mind"; one visitor-observer remarked that they are "more diverse than Amherst students." They reach out to "the world at large"; their "program in international education is one of their gems, and around 90 percent of the faculty have lived abroad .... Mennonite as it proudly is, Goshen is not divorced from the life of society at large ...." Yet the "apparent homogeneity" of Goshen's student body offers "little chance to tackle the unbelievers. To a visitor-observer, some students spoke of choosing Goshen so "they would be supported rather than beleaguered in their faith." And one "opined, 'Goshen doesn't preach Christianity enough; it only practices it.'" Some of the more evangelical students said that "the faculty are not confessional enough." Nonetheless, Goshen has made specific efforts to tie "the college and the churches together ...."

> —Paraphrased and quoted from Merrimon
> Cuninggim, 1978[2]

"It takes a strong church to have strong church schools."

> —Albert J. Meyer, Mennonite Board of
> Education, 2000[3]

Goshen College began at Elkhart, Indiana in 1894 as the "Elkhart Institute of Science, Industry, and the Arts." In the next decade it became more clearly collegiate and centered on the liberal arts, and in 1903 it moved to nearby Goshen and took its present name. That same decade ushered in the Progressive Era in American history, with its great faith that Americans could overcome the problems that new industry and burgeoning cities were bringing – and could live humanely. Goshen College was not isolated; both Elkhart and Goshen were and are in the main communication corridor running from the eastern cities to Chicago. The college began with much of the nation's mood of progressive optimism. In 1896 its main early shaper, an irenic and pastoral revivalist and church leader named John S. Coffman, favored the new school with a historic, ethos-breathing address he called "The Spirit of Progress."[4] In 1903, as Elkhart Institute's principal, Noah Byers, was inaugurated as president of the new, reconstituted Goshen College, Byers caught much the same mood in a speech titled "Culture for Service" – a phrase that caught on and became the college's enduring motto. For Byers and for the early Goshen the service idea was much informed by the then-current Protestant Student Volunteer Movement, with its slogan "evangelization of the world in this generation."[5] A strong motif was training missionaries and other workers for the Mennonite Church. It also had some overtones of Protestantism's version of progressivism, the social gospel, as sounded, for instance, in Goshen College leadership in forming an Intercollegiate Peace Society – which held its first convention on the campus in 1905.[6]

Yet even if affected by national moods, the new institution was a Mennonite college. By 1905 it became officially so, as the "old" (later called "MC") Mennonite branch formed a Board of Education and brought the school fully under denominational control. The Goshen story hardly fits standard analyses based on colleges and universities rooted in Calvinism and the Calvinist-informed national educational culture rooted in New England. Nor, for Goshen, does it quite work to use the paradigms of tension between historic Christian commitments and those of the 18th century's so-called Enlightenment.[7] Goshen did not pass through stages which historian George Marsden has proposed for America's previously Protestant or Protestant-dominated universities. By Marsden's reckoning, the time of Goshen's founding was one in which a moral-philosophy-oriented and culturally established Protestantism was losing dominance over higher education. In its place was coming a fusion of scientism and loose, eclectic Protestant liberalism.[8]

Mennonites' outlook transitions were different. In the 18th century, instead of fusing an establishment version of Christianity with Enlightenment rationalism, Mennonites were fusing a dissenting version of Christianity with a highly devotional, quietly experiential, and somewhat world-denying German Pietism.[9] And except within the wombs of Pennsylvania-German enclaves, Pietism reinforced an already strong over-against-culture sectarianism which Mennonites had inherited from their spiritual ancestors' persecution and suffering. Nor does Marsden's chronology apply to Mennonites. In the late 19th century the "old" Mennonites and the (non-Old Order) Amish Mennonites[10] were interacting not so much with scientism and modernism as with American revivalism.[11] Goshen College was a product of transition to greater revivalist-evangelical activism, not of the stages which Marsden identified for American universities.

From Goshen's beginning, Mennonites have seen their educational enterprise largely over against American thought and culture, not as a transmitter of that culture. To be sure, Mennonite educators have often looked to culture-dominating Protestantism for parts of their educational models; and modestly, they have, of course, interacted with the Enlightenment, science, and other themes of modern thought. But they have not made what Marsden identified as a common assumption in 19th-century universities: "that there should be a unified national culture in which the Protestant religion ought to play a major supportive part."[12] Instead, a strong theme of Mennonite intellectuals and college-builders has been that of counter-values and counterculture.

In 1991, apparently as a warning to all church-related colleges, University of Notre Dame theologian James Tunstead Burtchaell published an analysis of Vanderbilt University's gradual alienation from its founding Southern Methodist church. Along the way he observed that Vanderbilt's late-19th-century "youthful years" were precisely "a time when most Protestants lost conviction about the particularities" of their own respective denominations and reduced their Christianity to mere good citizenship and other hazy notions.[13] But Mennonites have remembered their particularities. In his "Spirit of Progress" speech, John S. Coffman connected themes such as progress, peace, and moral character not to national culture but to a tradition of, in his words, "dissenters from state churches." The dissenters he had in mind were 16th-century Anabaptists and a string of earlier breakaway groups.[14] Since Coffman's day, Mennonites and their educators have restated, even redefined their counterculturism; but running throughout Goshen's history is a continuous sense of distinct peoplehood, peculiar and dissenting.

Marsden closed one key article with the observation: "Perhaps … it is time for Christians in the post-modern age to recognize that they are part of an unpopular sect."[15] Apparently the point was an afterthought. Perhaps it should not have been. Perhaps Goshen's story could illuminate the larger national story after all.

Key Moments, Ideas and Themes in Goshen College History

Goshen's history, and to an extent the history of its church in the 20th century, is a tale of some high hopes, strong disappointments, but also stimuli – even some as unfortunate as global war – that in the end seemed to "work together for good to those who love the Lord."

1. Beginning to about 1918: a campus mood that was optimistic, oriented toward a Christian activism.

In its early years Goshen was imbued with a progressive, Protestant activist outlook. That combination seems to have attracted a good bevy of young people remarkable both in intellectual ability and in idealism.[16] As one had put it privately in 1893, such newly vitalized, progressive Mennonite youth were hoping to be "just the stuff."[17] In later years, quite a few erstwhile students of this optimistic era would look back upon the "old Goshen" as a kind of lost Eden.[18]

2. 1918-1924: a growing distance between academics and ecclesiastics, creating a crisis.

By 1923-1924 the Eden had withered: indeed, the college closed for one academic year. When it reopened it had a new administration, on the whole a new faculty, and, since quite a few "old Goshen" students refused to return, a somewhat altered student body. Powerful church leaders (as well as many ordinary Mennonites) had lost confidence in the college over issues of overexpansion, financial mismanagement, and, not least, fear of theological and cultural modernism. (It was, of course, the time when Protestant Fundamentalism's first wave was cresting. Once again, larger national and Protestant moods were affecting Mennonites – although with Mennonites the quarrels were as often about cultural matters, such as attire, as about doctrine.) On their side, a number of prominent faculty members, including President Byers and then his successor John E. Hartzler, moved – or, in the minds of many "old" Mennonites, defected – to the more flexible General Conference Mennonite branch and its colleges, Bluffton in Ohio and Bethel in Kansas.[19] Still, strong elements of the "old" Goshen pursued further acculturation and progressivism. College and church, "academics" and "ecclesiastics,"[20] were on diverging tracks. In that situation the college's form of government – control by a denomination-appointed board[21] — allowed the church to respond accordingly. The Board of Education acted, and for a year the college closed.

The situation was full of unforgettable tragedy: careers were interrupted; all too many students, including some highly able ones, were alienated from the "old" church and in some cases from Mennonitism of any kind (thankfully, some of the brightest and best eventually overcame this sense of alienation); scholarly freedom was compromised;[22] much faculty talent was lost to the church; and many relationships were broken. Nonetheless, from the perspective of bringing college and church back together and of maintaining church-related higher education, out of tragedy came considerable renewal.

3. 1924-1941: a "new" Goshen which was decidedly different, yet remained a liberal arts college, with considerable intellectual vigor.

Despite all its tragedy the 1923-1924 closing brought renewal, mainly from three sources: (1) strong and wise leaders in the college after the purge, especially the new president, Sanford C. Yoder, and the new dean, Noah Oyer; (2) a governing structure that simply would not let the college drift too far from its church connection; and (3) not least, underlying the first two reasons, a church whose sense of distinctiveness and peoplehood was so strong that persons on both sides of the college-versus-church divide decided that whatever the problems, they would stick together.

Sanford (S.C.) Yoder, an Iowan with a colorful background of homesteading in Washington state and earlier aspirations of being a lawyer (he was known to intrigue students with the admission that he had earlier used tobacco and still enjoyed the smell of a good cigar),[23] represented the best of the Amish Mennonite bishop as old-style elder and folk leader with shrewd understanding of the tribe's sociology and behaviors. During the closing, Yoder had been president of the college's governing board. Yet he was not a radical for the ecclesiastical side and after the reopening he quickly built confidence on campus – at least among persons loyal enough to return, including some with deep misgivings. At the time he became Goshen's president, he did not possess even a bachelor's degree. Yet he kept the institution academically respectable, as struggling young colleges go. Oyer, the new dean in 1924, had studied at Princeton Seminary before becoming a Bible teacher in another Mennonite institution. For such intellectual strength, Yoder was willing to take some risks – for instance, in 1924, .hiring a youthful Harold S. Bender, whose "soundness" was still in some doubt. Bender had studied at Goshen, Garrett, Princeton, and the University of Tübingen. In a few years he would became world Mennonitism's foremost intellectual leader.[24]

Yoder served as president through the rebuilding and then the Great Depression, until 1940. At first he often felt forced to use temporary teachers, and when he did, he seemed willing to engage non-Mennonites ahead of Mennonites whose intellectual qualifications or ultimate loyalty to church seemed doubtful.[25] By present standards the college suffered shaky finances and heavy demands for orthodoxy and orthopraxis, for instance asking prospective faculty, "Would you be willing to conform to the teaching and the practices of the Church in the matters of plainness of attire and general separation from the world?"[26] In 1931 the faculty and the board adopted – then put in every regular college catalog until 1970 – a firmly written, semi-fundamentalistic, 10-point statement of doctrine.[27] Nonetheless, in Yoder's years Goshen advanced academically to the point that in 1941 the North Central Association approved it for accreditation.

Indeed Goshen's intellectual climate was vigorous. In the mid-to-latter 1920s Harold S. Bender and several of his closest colleagues revived a Mennonite Historical Society, began what quickly became the respected international journal *The Mennonite Quarterly Review*, and inaugurated a scholarly, enduring book series, Studies in Anabaptist and Mennonite History. Most of all (building somewhat on groundwork laid by others),[28] they developed the "Anabaptist-vision" or "Goshen school" interpretation of the 16th-century Protestant Reformation – an interpretation so well accepted beyond Mennonite circles that by 1943 the American Society of Church History honored Bender with its presidency. Others who added to Goshen's vigorous intellectual climate included Bender's wife Elizabeth Horsch Bender, a German teacher and fine linguist and historian in her own right,[29] and Olive Wyse. Wyse, who in 1925 began a 50-year career of teaching at Goshen, mainly in home economics, won high intellectual respect from male colleagues – not automatic in those days – and later, in 1949, was a key writer of a new faculty statement of Goshen's educational philosophy.[30] Not least in the Yoder years and following was Guy F. Hershberger, a historian and sociologist who became, from the late 1930s to the 1960s, a (if not *the*) foremost interpreter of Mennonites' position on peace and other questions of church and society. By World War II Bender and Hershberger, with various fellow-Mennonite and other Historic Peace Church intellectuals, were key players in developing a national plan of alternative service for conscientious objectors to war.

In 1924 the "new" Goshen's governors had insisted on loyalty to the church. Perhaps they had carried loyalty to a fault; but clearly, a faculty so chosen served their church well, intellectually. And not only their church: by interpreting the history and sociology of a small dissenting group, and by helping formulate a plan by which government recognized conscientious objection far better than in World War I, they served the causes of humane tolerance, national pluralism, and human freedom.

4. World War II and following, to 1968: landmark writings on peace and Anabaptism, response to a global crisis, new ideology and practice of service.

World War II, of course, deeply impacted almost all Americans, individually and corporately. For Mennonites a considerable part of the impact came via the government-established but largely church-operated alternative service system for conscientious objectors, known as Civilian Public Service or "CPS." The system was a labyrinth that included forestry and other camps, agricultural extension assignments, mental hospital work, guinea-pig roles for medical research, and more. Some CPS draftees and some faculty members at Goshen and elsewhere helped administer it or conducted various educational programs in the various units. Meanwhile Mennonite leaders, including Goshen's new president, "old" Goshen graduate Ernest E. Miller, began to plan for vastly expanded wartime and postwar relief programs. Also growing were ideas for various church-sponsored programs of voluntary service. Amid such thinking, in 1943 the Goshen campus became the site of a Relief Workers Training School.[31] Goshen College's historian Susan Fisher Miller has detected in such wartime activities not only a strong interest in very specific forms of service but also some seeds of Goshen's later, widely recognized program of international education.[32]

Moreover, in mid-World War II as president of the American Society of Church History, Harold S. Bender delivered a historic address titled "The Anabaptist Vision." Its main ideas were that the Mennonites' religious forebears, the Anabaptists, had taken the lead in modern church-state separation; that they had carried the Protestant Reformation on to its logical conclusion; and that the essence of Anabaptism lay in three principles: believers' church, practical discipleship, and pacifistic love in human relations. Bender wrote the address hastily and for non-Mennonite scholars more than for his church, yet for Mennonites it somehow became a kind of manifesto for a postwar identity. In time "Anabaptist" identity became a Mennonite folk myth. Perhaps its power was that it allowed Mennonites to continue a strong sense of peoplehood and distinctiveness even as many began shedding older boundary-markers such as plain attire.

Older ideas of service remained strong, so that in the late 1940s and early 1950s the campus still honored students who chose missionary careers, and some did, including very talented ones.[33] In the county around Goshen the campus Young People's Christian Association (later "Student Christian Association") carried on evangelistic work that spawned a half-dozen new Mennonite congregations. For many Mennonites, not least the faculty and students at Goshen, the Anabaptist vision formula, by calling individuals to practical discipleship and love, easily reinforced the new war-stimulated emphasis on concrete forms of service. Also fueling the emphasis were the peace advocacy and social commentary of Guy F. Hershberger, culminating in two major books: *War, Peace and Nonresistance* (1944) and *The Way of the Cross in Human Relations* (1958).[34] One strong theme of Hershberger and others was preservation of the Mennonite community, and for a few years, beginning in 1947, a Mennonite Community Association published a *Mennonite Community* magazine.

"Anabaptist vision," new service emphasis, internationalism, community language, and theoretical rearticulations of Mennonitism and of at least one version of Mennonite pacifism: all these enriched Goshen's educational environment immeasurably. By the 1950s so many faculty members and spouses had done postwar relief service abroad that such experience seemed commonplace; by 1970, half of Goshen's faculty had served abroad (and not in military service).[35] Meanwhile a group of second-generation interpreters of the "Anabaptist vision" – most of whom had been students at Goshen or its related biblical seminary (including the eventually well known scholar John Howard Yoder) – added highly sophisticated critique and rigor to Mennonite thought and self-understanding. But the impact was felt more widely: a core group of young Mennonite intellectuals held various conferences with World Council of Churches leaders, Eastern European Marxists, and others, trying to bring a pacifist Christian perspective to the modern world's crises.[36] Meanwhile at Goshen and other Mennonite campuses in the 1950s, well before U.S. President John F. Kennedy's Peace Corps, it became common for students to put in a summer or two or three years of church-related voluntary service, either breaking into their college years or doing a term immediately after graduation. A church that had demanded loyalty of its college was now reaping ample benefits.

On campus, ideas clustered around terms and slogans such as "Anabaptist vision," "service," "community," and "peace." These themes ran through various courses not only in religion, ethics, and philosophy (some of which students had to take to meet general-education requirements) but in others such as history or literature as well. By the late 1950s a new watchword, "justice," began to emerge in a prominent way, especially on the lips and in the writings of philosophy professor and future Goshen president J. Lawrence Burkholder.[37] Goshen's service idealism found many forms: a pioneer liberal-arts-based nursing program with strong Christian-service emphasis;[38] an athletic program built around a conviction that it should be for fun and fitness, with modest intra- and inter-varsity activity (eventually including soccer as a pacifist form of football!), rather than an enterprise with its own win-at-any-cost values.[39] The music faculty, especially Professor Mary Oyer, contributed to church music by active leadership in compiling two major new hymnals produced cooperatively with other Anabaptist-derived groups, and by helping Mennonites make a transition to some use of instruments in worship while, at best, still preserving a strong a cappella tradition.[40] With a much-heralded fine arts course and by other means, Oyer and colleagues also helped Mennonites immeasurably to expand their limited appreciation for drama and the visual arts.[41]

The most thorough application of Goshen's core values to formal curricula came in 1968, when the college community began its now well-known program of sending the great majority of its students abroad, each for a full trimester, in a program soon labeled "SST," for "Study-Service Term." College historian Fisher Miller believed she found various roots of the SST idea: the early "Culture for Service" idea and motto; World War II and postwar service, including service abroad; a council of Mennonite college presidents' sponsorship of summer seminars abroad, some led by Goshen faculty members (beginning in 1963, a time of Peace Corps and other service idealism in national life); a milieu of expanding enrollments and general affluence; on campus, the work of a "Future of the College Committee" whom President Paul Mininger and Provost Henry Weaver, Jr. were challenging to dream new dreams; and not least, a visit in 1965 of a North Central Association accreditation team whose members asked why Goshen was not using its faculty's extensive international experience more effectively for its students' education.[42] Also, by this time Mennonites had a strong tradition of church-sponsored voluntary service, much of it abroad either under denominational agencies or under the leading interMennonite organization, Mennonite Central Committee (MCC). At the risk of making a false dichotomy it seems fair to say that Goshen's SST resulted more from the kind of church that sponsored the college than from the college itself.

In any case, since 1968 virtually every Goshen student has had to take, as part of the general education requirement, one term's worth of international studies. For some 80 percent[43] of the students that has meant a trimester or semester abroad in a unit of 12-25 fellow-students led by a Goshen faculty team (typically, but not always, a faculty member and spouse). The most notable features of the program are: inclusion in the regular curriculum, without large extra fees; organization around cross-cultural understanding and service even more than around language-learning; eschewing the world's centers of political, economic, and cultural power, instead locating in areas such as the Caribbean and Central America or a far-inland province of mainland China; units really run by Goshen faculty instead of simply attaching students to foreign universities with their special university cultures; and getting students to experience grass roots local culture by placing them with community agencies (schools, clinics, recreation programs, etc.), often in remote places, for half the term. Over time, the SST rationale of learning, relating, and functioning cross-culturally has probably surpassed the service idea per se.[44] Still, the service idea remains part of the program.

A sizable percentage of the faculty have led units abroad, usually for one year (three student groups). Student participation has gradually declined to about 70 percent,[45] yet students still obviously see the term abroad as a highlight. Some careful research strongly suggests that the program, along with the aura surrounding it, is effective pedagogically.[46] Goshen's identity and national reputation have become so tied to its international program that a few faculty members have asked whether, in the college's communal self-identity and values, international education has not moved above the Mennonite church connection. It is a fair question.

5. The generation since about 1970: various innovations, including new formulations of belief and goals; continued academic strength; continued strong relations with the Mennonite Church; but no ethos-changing developments.

Since the beginning of SST some innovations at Goshen have been imaginative enough, but quite a few have been mainly just to keep abreast of what the times demand. Certainly, Goshen College has retained or even increased some of its traditional strengths. As a teaching institution it is currently well-mentioned in guides such as *Barron's Best Buys in College Education, U.S. News & World Report's* list of "America's best colleges," and Erlene Wilson's *100 Best Colleges for African-American Students*. Of the 1,565 students who graduated from 1980 to 1985, 30 percent have reported receiving advanced degrees (36 percent if 670 who graduated from certain vocational majors[47] are not counted); and of 30 persons of the classes of 1988-1991 who applied to enter medical school, 83.3 percent were accepted. At present Goshen is the only Indiana college selected for the Pew Science Program in Undergraduate Education. Some of the institution's scholarly facilities have world reputations, especially: the Basil S. Turner Precision X-Ray Measurements Laboratory built up by Professor Robert C. Buschert, who clearly had chosen to be at Goshen because of core values; a Mennonite Historical Library; and *The Mennonite Quarterly Review*. Some other outstanding facilities and activities are: an extensive nature preserve with a vigorous program of environmental studies and demonstration; continued leadership in peace-related theory; and, of course, international education. One could offer various other examples.

On campus, the college has surely worked – although perhaps not hard enough – at more inclusion and better cross-cultural relations. It attracts quite a few international students (in 1999-2000, excluding 17 Canadians, 76 from 32 countries, in a student body of fewer than 1000). Since 1979 it has hosted a special church-sponsored program to train leaders for Hispanic congregations. It has been somewhat less successful at incorporating American minorities into its regular program and at improving cross-cultural relations on campus; but in 1992 various earlier efforts metamorphosed into a new Multicultural Education Office, which provides vigorous leadership toward those ends.[48] On quite a different subject, sexuality, both campus and church have had strong leadership from Willard S. Kraybill, college physician and health teacher (now retired); and since 1989 the college's Student Development Division has furnished each student with a set of documents making up a "sexuality packet" or "sexuality insert" in orientation materials. Sexuality issues sometimes strain college-church relations (but hardly more than relations within each entity); yet surely the packet is a creative effort to articulate standards and to effect them by education, by counseling, and by instilling inner values, rather than by legalism. Any lack of clarity about sexuality is an ambiguity the college shares with its church.

Goshen College is not resting on its laurels. Nonetheless, since the early 1970s much creative energy has gone into just "keeping up." Enrollments are somewhat below previous peaks, and rightly or wrongly, the college has not chosen to attract students by offering an overtly aggressive evangelical or other high-profile religious program. (The college's 1980-82 catalog, trying to communicate a purely noncoercive and service-oriented approach to faith, even noted that Goshen College dormitories did not have "officially sponsored Bible studies or sharing times.") Nor has the institution tried to sell itself as a culturally safe haven.[49] Meanwhile modern financial demands plus the costs of operating SST have strained the efforts to stay abreast; even a donor's $26 million endowment gift in 1993 was no magic solution, especially with sometimes-anemic enrollments keeping tuition revenues down. Recent expenditures such as putting up-to-date computers on every faculty desk and paving parking lots for resident students may be in some sense "necessary," yet they hardly improve *quality* of education. Some other changes such as excellent computer laboratories, a multi-million dollar recreation-and-fitness center opened in 1994, and a new music facility now under construction, surely do relate to improving education. Yet a strong motive is "just keeping up."

As for the church connection, since 1970 there have been efforts to renew the church's sense of ownership of the college and to restate the essence of what Goshen College aims to be. One fruit of the early years of the administration of J. Lawrence Burkholder, president from 1971 to 1984, was a plan, now quite widely accepted in the denomination, whereby congregations subsidize the tuition of their youths who choose a Mennonite institution. As for essence, in the early 1970s the college replaced that 1931 doctrinal statement. Already in 1949 the faculty had formulated a "Concept of Christian Education at Goshen College" expressed very much in early-postwar "Anabaptist-vision" and service language.[50] For a time in the 1970s the college catalog offered a five- or six-point statement that, while still quite doctrinal, was doctrinal in a more "Anabaptist-vision" idiom.[51] Since 1970, catalog statements have been less doctrinal and more like conversations around certain concepts. Typical ones: "peace," "discipleship," and "service," plus "community," "caring," and wholistic education.

Since the 1970s Goshen's faculty and its board have applied considerable creativity to producing new statements of mission and objectives. In its short form, the current mission statement states:

> Goshen College is a four-year liberal arts college dedicated to the development of informed, articulate, sensitive, responsible Christians. As a ministry of the Mennonite Church, we seek to integrate Christian values with educational and professional life. As a community of faith and learning, we strive to foster personal, intellectual, spiritual and social growth. We view education as a moral activity that produces servant-leaders for the church and the world.

A longer form of the mission statement includes some more church-related language, such as "encouraging active participation and leadership in congregations" and accepting "Jesus Christ as Son of God, as Lord of Life, and as Savior from the bondage of sin." It also uses some more distinctly Anabaptist-Mennonite language; and it affirms the Mennonite Church statements of faith. There are other documents, including a major 1994 statement whose subheadings include "a vital community of learning"; "Christian faith"; "service and peacemaking"; and "diversity and global awareness." The "Christian faith" section is not creedal. Along with its mission statement the college designates ten "desired outcomes."[52]

In all, the several statements do not emphasize the kind of orthodoxy under which the early "new Goshen" regrouped. For instance, the 1994 statement mentions "Spirit" but not scripture. One might ask, is Goshen College presently in a mode much like one of George Marsden's stages after all – the Liberal Protestant one?[53] Whatever the answer, even the mission and outcomes statements have a strong element of "keeping abreast" – abreast of "management by objective" methods and of the approach demanded by the college's accrediting agency. Since the beginning of the SST program, there have been some worthwhile innovations but none of these has established a new ethos for the coming decades.

Reflections

Goshen's church relationship has remained strong. With the governing pattern established in 1905, the college simply would not be left to itself. More fundamentally, the explanation for Goshen's strong church ties lies not so much with the college itself as with the kind of church to which Goshen College relates. The crux is a church with a strong enough sense of its own place in God's scheme and a strong enough sense of peoplehood that its various members, including its academics, hang together, "for better or for worse," to fulfill that place.

If one seeks to understand Goshen College, one must understand several other dimensions as well.

1. Goshen's place in higher education rests more on what it and its people have *done* than on *words* or *theory*. Running through

Goshen's documents there are indeed some persistent words, having to do with building "character," teaching a faith to permeate all of life, educating the whole person, fostering personal development and growth, and of course educating in the context of faith. But Goshen has been spare with words. A persistent theme of J. Lawrence Burkholder during his presidency was that Goshen College has tended to make its case by understatement and that the college was "authentic."[54] Mennonites tend to search for truth far less in words or abstract systems than in practice.[55] Perhaps for that reason the college and its church have not produced many notable statements of educational theory.

In 1992 Goshen's president, Victor Stoltzfus, used a three-month sabbatical to probe the literature and several key examples of church-related colleges, and wrote a small book on the subject. In sum he offered five points which offer something of an educational philosophy: "the church-affiliated college should serve the students and parents of the founding denomination ..."; it also should offer "ecumenical sensitivity" for other students; it should teach the liberal arts as "classic wisdom tested by the centuries"; it "should be a 'salt and light' model institution, credible to nation and world and "intellectually engaged with the cutting edge of intellectual and policy issues of the secular society ..."; and, "in gratitude for the indirect public support which it enjoys from the state and nation," it should engage in "public service."[56] There have been other statements: catalog statements, a 121-page "Religious Welfare Survey Report"[57] compiled by Goshen faculty in 1947-1949;[58] faculty attempts to integrate faith and particular disciplines;[59] and the like. But in 1968 historian Paton Yoder, charged by Mennonite Church leaders with reviewing their denomination's educational philosophy, found none of the attempts very impressive.[60] The same seems true for most of the period since he wrote. For instance, a 1971 booklet with the subtitle *A Philosophy of Education for the Mennonite Church* was replete with code words such as "community" and with good common sense ("the values taught to the young must be practiced by adults"), but it hardly offered the sustained, systematic reasoning implied in the word "philosophy."[61] But it did and does express the general Mennonite approach.

2. Despite the 1923-1924 closing, Goshen has *not* faced a church or a governing board that was (as Burtchaell found in Vanderbilt's

case) "unrelievedly negative."[62] Even during the 1923-1924 closing, by keeping Sanford Yoder as chair of the governing board the Mennonite Church showed that it was interested in reconstructing the college, not destroying it. And current figures on contributions from the church to the college show considerable support. Of annual contributions to Goshen College each year, about 20 percent are from the Mennonite Church as church. Much of the other 80 percent, including that from alumni, business, and industry, also is from Mennonites. This 80 percent also reflects strong church-college connections; according to Mennonite understandings of church, however, "church support" must mean considerable support from the church corporately, not only individual-by-individual.

3. Neither has the college ever moved into one mode that Marsden and Burtchaell found typical in higher education's "secularization": that of cutting denominational ties while still claiming to be generically Christian – indeed claiming, as Burtchaell paraphrased, to be more "authentically" and "wisely" Christian than before.[63] Goshen has not gone that route. If it did, it probably would become a "generic peace college." Goshen's public rhetoric has indeed changed, and writers such as Marsden and Burtchaell would certainly find a "blurring of nomenclature"[64] or "rhetorical slide."[65] Especially since 1970 the college's catalogs have become more breezy and more oriented to language of personal and relational development when compared to crisper statements of commitment and belief.[66] Increasingly, Goshen fits a label which Stoltzfus applied to certain Catholic schools: "Humane Values colleges."[67] However good that character, Goshen's people might do well to ponder a point which Marsden strongly implied and Burtchaell stated forthrightly: that "*it has been active Christians, not hostile secularists, who were most effective in alienating the colleges and universities from their communities of faith.*"[68]

The change in Goshen's idiom, if it might seem to reflect Marsden's "Liberal Protestant" stage, has not led to that stage's typically devastating effect on church-college relations. By the definitions of strong college-church relatedness which come from another quarter, namely those put forward by Merrimon Cuninggim in a 1978 National Council of Churches study, Goshen's change in public rhetoric does not necessarily imply a weakening of relationship to the church; it may actually reflect parallel developments within leading elements of the

Mennonite Church itself. Some commentators may think that the case is one of downward slide for both college and church; others may think not. In either case, college and church seem to be moving hand-in-hand.

4. One way that Goshen has kept a clear relationship to its church is by having board members 100 percent Mennonite, permanent faculty either Mennonite or highly sympathetic, and at least 65 percent of the students Mennonite. Some faculty and other interested parties are apt to think that relaxing the Mennonite student percentage might help Goshen's enrollment. Others have pointed to losses in Mennonite recruitment: since 1980, "MC" Mennonite students in Mennonite colleges have declined from about 1750 to 1350 per year, while those in non-Mennonite institutions have increased from about 1750 to 2900. Why, some ask, are Goshen and other Mennonite colleges not attracting so many of their own? Viewed individual-by-individual, the 65 percent rule certainly seems arbitrary.[69] Mennonites themselves are diverse, and the presence of other students clearly enriches the educational climate. Why make Mennonite-relatedness a criterion?

A college's students – not only its faculty, administration, boards, and philosophy – do much to set the educational climate. The percentage rule rests on a logic of thresholds, or "critical mass." For present-day Mennonites the practical question seems to be how to find the optimum (and biblical) mix of both "distinctive community" and inclusivism. For Goshen College it seems to be, Where is the threshold beyond which diversity brings a loss of the institution's purposes and character? In the aggregate, to assume no correlation between being Mennonite and fostering an educational climate that fits the church's and the college's values is to say that Mennonite rearing or membership means nothing. If that is true, then why any relationship of college and church at all?

Much the same is true of faculty, as Albert J. Meyer notes in his closing essay in this volume. In choosing faculty, Goshen College does not now impose, or want, rigid uniformity. Mennonite faculty themselves by no means all think alike, and at present a sprinkling of faculty who are other than Mennonite are well-integrated into campus life, enriching it. But again, individual-by-individual thinking is not adequate for policy. Goshen College's policy is that "all faculty members" are "expected to be active participants and members of Mennonite or other Christian congregations and in full sympathy with the doctrines and practices of the Mennonite Church."[70]

In recent years, former president Victor Stoltzfus strengthened the steps and requirements for faculty candidates to express their faith and its meaning for the positions they seek.[71] Burtchaell observed that at some point Vanderbilt University "lost the ability to affirm in the first person plural that it was Methodist."[72] Quite apart from governance, the student quota, faculty composition, and other formalities, what does it take for Goshen's people to "affirm in the first person plural" that we are Mennonite?

5. Finally, a subtle issue of commitment versus relativism needs to be addressed. Do Goshen's embracing of pluralism and its promotion of cross-cultural understanding imply a relativism of a kind that can undermine real faith commitment? The intent of the question certainly is not to diminish appreciation for the intrinsic values of pluralism and cross-culturalism; and as led by its director Zenebe Abebe, Goshen's Multicultural Education Office clearly works from faith-commitment, not relativism. As with Jesus' choice of disciples, the bringing together of different people across various divides is itself a strong Christian value. On this matter, too, college and church seem to be moving together, if one can judge by recent language coming out of the Mennonite Church. The question's intent is only to ask whether pursuing one set of excellent goals might have a side-effect which deserves more attention: temptation toward a faith-corroding relativism. Most notably: Is Goshen communicating well enough to students and others that its heralded SST program rests on faith commitments? Is the message clearly to invite faith commitment, rather than a relativism that might make all faith commitments seem like mere cultural expression?

Conclusion

Much in the "failure" literature of church-college relations – the literature analyzing increasing "secularization" – does not apply well to Goshen. Goshen has not identified fundamentally with national culture, nor has it developed mainly out of struggles with Enlightenment thinking or with science. Yet the main strength of its Mennonite Church relationship rests not on that negative, but on a positive: thus far, both the Mennonite Church and Goshen College have maintained a strong enough sense of purpose and peoplehood

33

to keep their church-college relationship intact. Underlying such purpose and peoplehood have been Mennonites' traditions of countercultural dissent. Still, Goshen's church and faith connections deserve constant reflection. Far from being set over against one another, Goshen College and its church still seem able to ask the questions together. For the two to continue asking the questions together seems to depend as much on what kind of church the Mennonite Church will continue to be as on the college itself. "It takes a strong church to have strong church schools."

---

1. Theron F. Schlabach, Professor of History at Goshen College, is active in research and writing and occasional teaching. This essay is adapted slightly from "Goshen College and Its Church Relations: History and Reflections," in Richard T. Hughes and William B. Adrian, eds., *Models for Christian Higher Education: Strategies for Success in the Twenty-First Century* (Grand Rapids: William B. Eerdmans, 1997), 200-221.

2. From Merrimon Cuninggim, "Varieties of Church-Relatedness in Higher Education," Section I of Robert Rue Parsonage, ed., *Church Related Higher Education: Perceptions and Perspectives* (Valley Forge: Judson Press, 1878), 52-54.

3. See Meyer's chapter in this volume.

4. J[ohn]. S. Coffman, *The Spirit of Progress: A Lecture, Delivered at the Opening of the First School Building of the "Elkhart Institute," Elkhart, Ind., Feb. 11, 1896* (booklet in Mennonite Historical Library, Goshen College [hereafter MHL]). Coffman was the Mennonite Church's leading revivalist; at the time of the speech he was about to become president of the new school's governing board. Not only the speech's title but much of its content fit the rhetoric of the times. For example, Coffman suggested (18) that the world's leaders were beginning to honor the Prince of Peace – but then so had Daniel Coit Gilman, founder of Johns Hopkins University, in a speech to Protestant church leaders in 1887; see George M. Marsden, "The Soul of the American University: A Historical Overview," ch. 1 in Marsden and Bradley J. Longfield, eds., *The Secularization of the Academy* (New York: Oxford University Press, 1992), 17.

5. Susan Fisher Miller, *Culture for Service: A History of Goshen College, 1894-1994* (Goshen: Goshen College, 1994), 44, 24-25. Fisher Miller noted (44) that Byers gave his "Culture for Service" speech and coined the motto soon after Columbia University's President Nicholas Murray Butler had given a speech on "Scholarship for Service," but suggested that Byers put his own meaning into the words. In 1896 Woodrow Wilson, future president of Princeton University, gave a major address titled "Princeton in the Nation's Service"; see Richard Hofstadter and Wilson Smith, *American Higher Education: A Documentary History* (Chicago: University of Chicago Press, 1961), II, 684-95. The service idea is a main theme of a book by Mark Noll on Princeton University's early history; that fact and the Woodrow Wilson reference are reported in Marsden, "The Soul," 19, 43n.17.

6. John Sylvanus Umble, *Goshen College, 1894-1954: A Venture in Christian Higher Education* (Goshen: Goshen College, 1955), 45-46.

7. A framework suggested, e.g., in Richard Hughes, "Models for Christian Higher Education: Strategies for Survival and Success in the 21st Century" (unpublished grant proposal to Lilly Foundation underlying the study which resulted in the text in which this essay originally appeared), 1.

8. Marsden, "The Soul," 9-45.

9. See esp. ch. 6 of Richard K. MacMaster, *Land, Piety, Peoplehood: The Making of Mennonite Communities in America, 1683-1790*, The Mennonite Experience in America vol. 1 (Scottdale: Herald Press, 1985).

10. The statement does not refer to the Old Order Amish, but instead to a much larger number of Amish who were more progressive, worked closely with the "old" Mennonite church, and then in the 1910s and 1920s merged into the latter and lost the Amish name; see Steven M. Nolt, *A History of the Amish* (Intercourse: Good Books, 1992), chs. 7-8.

11. This transition has been a major subject of my own studies, in: "Reveille for *Die Stillen im Lande*: A Stir Among Mennonites in the Late Nineteenth Century," *The Mennonite Quarterly Review* [hereafter *MQR*] 51 (July 1977), 213-26; "The Humble Become Aggressive Workers: Mennonites Organize for Mission, 1880-1910," *MQR* 52 (Apr. 1978), 113-26; or much the same data and analysis in ch. 1 of my *Gospel Versus Gospel: Mission and the Mennonite Church, 1863-1944*, Studies in Anabaptist and Mennonite History no. 21 (Scottdale: Herald Press, 1980). For the ethos of 19th-century Mennonitism before the absorption of revivalist activism, see esp.: Joseph C. Liechty, "Humility: The Foundation of Mennonite Religious Outlook in the 1860s," *MQR* 54 (Jan. 1980), 5-31; and my *Peace, Faith, Nation: Mennonites and Amish in Nineteenth-Century America*, The Mennonite Experience in America vol. 2 (Scottdale: Herald Press, 1988), esp. chs. 1 and 4 (and for the new activism, ch. 11).

12. Marsden, "The Soul," 30.

13. James Tunstead Burtchaell, "The Decline and Fall of the Christian College," *First Things: A Monthly Journal of Religion and Public Life* (April-May 1991), 28.

14. Coffman, *Spirit of Progress*, 9.

15. Marsden, "The Soul," 41; see also Burtchaell, "Decline and Fall," 38.

16. Generalizations such as this one I make from the background of a fair amount of research, writing, and teaching history of Mennonites in the United States – and from Susan Fisher Miller's *Culture for Service*, cited above. A strong feature of Fisher Miller's book is skillful communication of campus ethos in different eras.

17. George (G.L.) Bender, quoted in Schlabach, *Gospel Versus Gospel*, 43.

18. Susan Fisher Miller, in conversation on 28 December 1994, used the term "lost Eden" or something close to it.

19. Fisher Miller, *Culture for Service*, chs. 3 and 4, esp. 51, 61, 69, 74-81; James C. Juhnke, *Vision, Doctrine, War: Mennonite Identity and Organization in America, 1890-1930* (Scottdale: Herald Press, 1989), 264-65; A. Warkentin and Melvin Gingerich, *Who's Who Among the Mennonites* (North Newton: A. Warkentin, 1943), 37, 44, 99, 224, 272.

20. The analysis of "academics" versus "ecclesiastics" is from Fisher Miller, *Culture for Service*, ch. 4.

21. Not, however, control by central denominational officers. In the "old" Mennonite church, major power and sovereignty lay with district conferences. The district conferences, both "old" Mennonite and Amish Mennonite, appointed members of the Mennonite Board of Education. For a quick review of the history of governance in American church-affiliated higher education, see Victor Stoltzfus, *Church-Affiliated Higher Education: Exploratory Case Studies of Presbyterian, Roman Catholic and Wesleyan Colleges* (Goshen: Pinchpenny Press, 1992), 39-46.

22. Fisher Miller, *Culture for Service*, 117.

23. Fisher Miller, *Culture for Service*, 177-78.

24. On how fortunate were the choices of Oyer and Bender, see Fisher Miller, *Culture for Service*, esp. 128-29, 133-34, 136-37, 147-50.

25. Fisher Miller, *Culture for Service*, 131-32.

26. Quoted in Fisher Miller, *Culture for Service*, 126.

27. Goshen College catalogs, issued usually biennially as March, April, or May issues of the *Goshen College Bulletin*, 25-64 (1931-1970). In structure and some content, the statement certainly smacked of Protestant Fundamentalist creeds (scriptural inerrancy as its first point, Christ's death as a "substitutionary sacrifice," literal resurrection not only of Jesus Christ but also "of all men," etc.). Yet it omitted some of the strongest Fundamentalist code words, e.g., "plenary and verbal" for scriptural inspiration; it certainly did not specify premillenialism; and it incorporated special Mennonite emphases, notably "discipleship," "non-resistance to evil by carnal means," and "nonconformity to the world in life and conduct" (but surprisingly did not specify nonconformity in attire).

28. See Al Keim, "The Anabaptist Vision: The History of a New Paradigm," *The Conrad Grebel Review* 12 (Fall 1994), 243-45, 247-49, 252.

29. See a special issue of *The Mennonite Quarterly Review* honoring her: 60 (July 1986).

30. Fisher Miller, *Culture for Service*, 138; conversation with Wyse's colleague Robert C. Buschert, 26 December 1994.

31. Fisher Miller, *Culture for Service*, 168, 172.

32. Fisher Miller, *Culture for Service*, 168. For more on Goshen's Study-Service Term, see below and other references throughout this volume, especially Wilbur J. Birky's brief essay.

33. Reminiscence of Robert C. Buschert, who was a student and then instructor at Goshen during that era. One hesitates to single out any of those mission-bound students, but it would be easy to name examples of extremely talented persons choosing mission work.

34. For a handy sketch of Hershberger and his thought and activity, see my "To Focus a Mennonite Vision," in John Richard Burkholder and Calvin Redekop, eds., *Kingdom Cross and Community: Essays on Mennonite Themes in Honor of Guy F. Hershberger* (Scottdale: Herald Press, 1976), 15-50.

35. *Goshen College Bulletin* (Mar. 1969), 4.

36. See Beulah Stauffer Hostetler, "Nonresistance and Social Responsibility: Mennonites and the Mainline Peace Emphasis, ca. 1950 to 1985," *MQR* 64 (Jan. 1990), 49-73, esp. 49-58; Donald F. Durnbaugh, ed., *On Earth Peace: Discussions on War/Peace Issues Between Friends, Mennonites, Brethren and European Churches, 1935-1975* (Elgin: The Brethren Press, 1978).

37. One could cite various articles by Burkholder; his fullest statement is J.

Lawrence Burkholder, *The Problem of Social Responsibility from the Perspective of the Mennonite Church* (Elkhart: Institute of Mennonite Studies, 1989), actually written as its author's 1958 Ph.D. dissertation at Princeton Theological Seminary.

38. See esp. "Forty Years of Nursing Education at Goshen College" (extended brochure of the Goshen College Department of Nursing [ca. 1993]).

39. See *Goshen College Bulletin* (Mar. 1972).

40. Some material in this paragraph comes simply from my own memories: I was a student at Goshen 1956-1960, kept in close touch during my graduate studies 1960-1965, and since 1965 have been on Goshen's faculty. Various faculty members – some of them with even longer histories at Goshen than I, read and commented on an earlier, longer draft of this chapter.

41. Conversation with Anne Hershberger, 2 March 1994. Notable events were conferences of Mennonite visual artists drawn together at exhibitions on the Goshen campus in 1975 and 1980 (the first one self-consciously a part of the 450th anniversary of Anabaptism's founding). See two volumes of reproductions from those exhibitions: Abner Hershberger, comp., *Mennonite Artists Contemporary 1975 and Mennonite Artists Contemporary 1980* (both, Goshen: Goshen College; years indicated).

42. Fisher Miller, *Culture for Service*, 168, 246-47.

43. Estimate by Wilbur Birky, Goshen's director of international education, who said also that the late-1990s figure is more like 70 per cent – but that both figures would be considerably higher if one counted all persons not specifically in SST but getting academic recognition for other activities abroad.

44. Possibly a false dichotomy: increasingly, Mennonite "service" leaders see cross-cultural relating and functioning as themselves a form of service.

45. See note 43.

46. See Norman L. Kauffmann, "The Impact of Study Abroad on Personality Change" (Ed.D. dissertation, Indiana University, 1983). A book using data from several institutions is Norman L. Kauffmann, Judith N. Martin, and Henry D. Weaver, with Judy Weaver, *Students Abroad: Strangers at Home: Education for a Global Society* (Yarmouth: Intercultural Press, 1992), 194.

47. Accounting, Business, Elementary or Middle School Education, Hispanic Ministries, Nursing, Social Work.

48. See Chandron Fernando, "GC Looks Back: Intercultural Efforts Grow, Adapt over Time," *Goshen College Multicultural Affairs Newsletter* 3 (Fall 1994), 8.

49. Quotation is from *Goshen College Catalog* 1980-82, 10 – quite a remarkable page for expressing the college's idea of religious emphasis. The college has supported pursuit of faith in quite a number of ways, including required Bible and religion courses and required attendance at either chapel (clearly worship) or convocations (not worship, but sometimes with religious elements). But especially in the last generation, most other explicit faith-promoting efforts are low-key and rest quite heavily on student initiative: pastoral counseling services, encouragement to choose from the local smorgasbord of Mennonite and other church congregations, and quiet support of students' own worship services or fellowship groups. As for a cultural "safe haven," since about 1970 a statement of "Standards for Guiding Our Life Together" has been the basis for promoting responsible behavior and for bringing sanctions against various substance, sexual, and other deviances. Substance violations include any possession or use not only of illegal drugs but also of alcohol,

either on campus or in other college-approved group settings. They also include use of tobacco anywhere on campus. Since the mid-1970s Goshen has had extensive hours allowing inter-gender dormitory visits and some inter-gender housing. Students also have access to a host of cable channels piped into campus and free access to any Internet resources. Conscientious students appreciate an atmosphere that clearly proscribes or strongly discourages various behaviors which occur quite openly on many American campuses; but Goshen does not, and honestly could not, tout itself strongly as a culturally safe haven.

50. *Goshen College Bulletin: Catalog for 1950-51* 44 (Mar. 1950).

51. *Goshen College Catalog 1976-78.*

52. They are: "faith that is active and reflective;" "intercultural openness with the ability to function effectively with people of other world views"; "the ability to communicate effectively in a variety of sign systems"; "the ability to think actively and strategically"; "an understanding of the transcendent reality of aesthetic and spiritual experience"; "personal integrity that fosters ability to resolve conflict and to promote justice"; "leadership ability that empowers self and others"; "an understanding of responsible stewardship for human systems and the environment"; "a sense of vocational direction"; and "a healthy understanding of self and others that is reflected in social relationships of interdependence and mutual accountability."

53. It seems quite clear that if authors such as Marsden and Burtchaell would compare recent mission, vision, and desired-outcomes statements to Goshen's earlier statements of belief, they would see "secularization." It seems equally clear that the statements would cause no alarm with persons who produced the Parsonage-edited 1978 National Council of Churches' *Church Related Higher Education.* Although the Parsonage report does set up an eight-point test of church-relatedness (74-84), in the spirit of modern American pluralism it celebrates the many ways colleges may express their church-relatedness and rejects as mythical any great use of doctrinal tests; see esp. its ch. 1. Small wonder, then, that (in their description at the outset of this chapter) the study's observers and writers were so positive about Goshen College.

54. E.g., Burkholder statements in: *Goshen College Catalog 1978-80; Goshen College Bulletin* (July 1979).

55. To quite a degree, some Mennonites' extensive flirtation with Protestant Fundamentalism in this century is an exception; but even there, the Mennonite version of Fundamentalism put great emphasis on practical nonconformity, nonresistance, and other evidences in day-to-day life. One might argue with some cogency that the "Anabaptist vision" was a verbal formula; but while the founders of the "Goshen school" often took pains to declare their Christian orthodoxy, their message rested on an interpretation of actual history, not on systematic theology.

56. Stoltzfus, *Church-Affiliated Higher Education,* 112-13.

57. Goshen College, Religious Welfare Survey Committee, "Religious Welfare Survey Report" (multilithed, n.d. [1949]). Available in MHL.

58. Paton Yoder, "Toward a Mennonite Philosophy of Higher Education Since 1890" (multilithed "Philosophy of Christian Education Study for the Mennonite Church: Workshop Paper C," 13-16 September 1968, Hesston, Kansas,), 50. Available in MHL.

59. Yoder, "Toward a Mennonite Philosophy," 48.

60. Yoder, "Toward a Mennonite Philosophy," 48.

61. Daniel Hertzler and others, *Mennonite Education: Why and How? A Philosophy of Education for the Mennonite Church* (booklet, Scottdale: Herald Press, 1971); quotation, 19.

62. Burtchaell, "Decline and Fall," 26.

63. Burtchaell, 24; see also Marsden, "The Soul," 27.

64. Phrase in Burtchaell, "Decline and Fall," 27.

65. Phrase in Meyer, "Mennonite Colleges," 16. In using the phrase, Meyer (the Mennonite Board of Education's former top executive and leading theorist) was paraphrasing Burtchaell, not referring to Mennonite colleges; but he was warning Mennonite educators against "a gradually-increasing vagueness and lack of specificity" in their religious-commitment language.

66. Generalization based on survey of the college's catalogs, 1896-1992.

67. Stoltzfus, *Church-Affiliated Higher Education*, 21.

68. Burtchaell, "Decline and Fall," 29.

69. The last two sentences echo discussions in Goshen faculty meetings in the fall and winter of 1994-1995. The statistics on attendance patterns are from the Mennonite Board of Education.

70. "Goshen College Faculty Handbook" (Nov. 1993), section 7.1.

71. Conversation with Stoltzfus, 25 January 1995. See the form he used when interviewing candidates for full- and part-time faculty positions.

72. Burtchaell, "Decline and Fall," 27.

3

DISCOVERING AN ANABAPTIST VOICE:
A PHILOSOPHY OF EDUCATION

Shirley Hershey Showalter[1]

"I have been my whole life a bell and never knew
it until at that moment I was lifted and struck."

—Annie Dillard, Pilgrim at Tinker Creek[2]

The day I first read those words of Annie Dillard, I was 32 years old.
The date was 1981. I had the luxury of "deep time," and I was reading for pleasure in Port au Prince, Haiti, where my husband Stuart
and I were leading a group of students in Goshen's Study-Service
Term. I felt a frisson – a shiver – in that 90-degree heat that I never
forgot. From that moment on, my education could be described as
paying attention to the moments I have been lifted and struck and
becoming aware that the great desire of my heart is to be united with
other bells, a choir of other voices, first on this earth and then in the
life to come.

A second essay which contributed much to my education was
H.S. Bender's "The Anabaptist Vision,"[3] which Theron Schlabach

addressed in his historical essay in this volume. I won't tell you how many years I read about Bender's vision and heard about the text before I finally read it. When I did, I had one of those "bell moments" – this one a tinkling brass. One of my memories of my own undergraduate years in the late 1960s was hearing one of my favorite Eastern Mennonite College professors, Herbert Martin, proclaim with glee that he loved to refinish old furniture because when he finally got down to the original wood, he always felt like he was recovering the Anabaptist vision. At the time, more than 30 years ago, I could tell by his tone that he was being both reverent and irreverent. And the comment stuck with me. But I had to come to Goshen, a decade later, and learn about Harold Bender before I could understand Herbert Martin. In the process I learned something about influence. Whoever speaks a definitive word will be affectionately mocked even as we scrub for the new truth. And it will become clear eventually that another word must be spoken.

Such is the way of the bell. On my last sabbatical, full of the bliss that only sabbaticals produce, I wrote a little poem called "The Purpose of the Bell." It ends with the words, "After the singing, the silence." Actually, T.S. Eliot said it much better: "Words, after speech, reach into the silence."

The day has passed in the Mennonite Church when one essay can create *the* definitive word. We are living in the age of multiple, contending voices and stories. If we proclaim the Truth with a capital "T," some thoughtful graduate student will be sure to correct us. One of our graduates recently wrote to me announcing that he would be taking a seminar with philosopher Jacques Derrida. I was excited with him, and I was touched by his desire to share the reading list for the course, which included several biblical texts. I challenged this Pew Evangelical Scholar alumnus to find meaning in the fact that our understanding of meaning itself is changing.

We need not carry the burden of the capital "T" in Truth. God can handle that job. But we must find the capital "T" of our own truth. Before that happens, we have to be lifted and struck.

I was struck, upon rereading chapters by Mennonites Rod Sawatsky, Theron Schlabach, and Paul Toews in Richard Hughes and William Adrian's *Models for Christian Higher Education*,[4] with a theme that runs through each. It could be understood as a theme of lament. I shall call it the problem of silence. In his essay, Sawatsky quotes historian James Juhnke, who wrote that "none of the early college leaders set forth a truly coherent philosophy of Mennonite education."[5] Schlabach's reflections, also included in this volume, include a similar statement: "Goshen's place in higher education rests more on what it and its people have done than on words or theory."[6] And finally, Paul Toews notes that Fresno Pacific College's origins as a Bible college meant that it focused on training rather than education.[7] While his account does not comment on a lack of philosophy and theology, as Sawatsky and Schlabach both do, it does not supply one either.

I would like to turn this potential lament and observed absence into an exploration of what I think is a real presence – a real presence which needs to become even more real in the years ahead. Now is the time for the unheard voice of my great-grandmother Emma Brubaker Snyder and all of our grandmothers. Now is the time to hear the voices of people whose ancestry is African, and Asian, and Hispanic. Now is the time for us to bring these voices into dialogue with the thousands of 16th-century martyrs in Europe. Now is the time to find new names for what we have learned and offer new names to our students. Now is the time to build on all those characteristics of incarnational education Rod Sawatsky offered us[8] and to seek many different kinds of language. We need the analytical and systematic, but we also need the language of prayer and poetry and painting and peacemaking. We should build our language from our experience, not work from the proposition to application. We have been given the gift of an incarnational approach to education. Now is the time to name that gift. Now is the time to bring many voices into the circle. Now is the time to sing.

I believe we are all living in the same kind of moment that Paul Toews described at Fresno Pacific in the early 1960s: "It was indeed a propitious moment – one given to few generations – when the future is open, when the dominant institutions and values of the past are clearly on the skids but the shape of the new is not yet clear."[9]

Several summers ago I was invited to the home of Wellesley President Diana Chapman Walsh after we had been introduced by a mutual friend, Parker Palmer. The verandah setting, overlooking the Charles River, brought to my mind another meeting – that of novelist Sarah Orne Jewett and the young writer Willa Cather at 148 Charles Street, Boston. Even though their meetings in person were infrequent, Jewett offered an example and advice that produced new depth and resonance in Willa Cather's voice as a writer. Cather's biographers often quote the sentence that Cather herself singled out as "one of the few helpful words" she had ever heard "from an older writer": "Of course, one day you will write about your own country. In the meantime, get all you can. One must know the world *so well* before one can know the parish."[10]

My own voice has benefited greatly by listening to other educators in higher education today. The more I listen and read, the more convinced I am that we have something precious in our parish at Goshen College, and that to understand it we need to understand the rest of the world "so well." From friends at a distance we can receive vision – for that is what vision is – long-distance seeing. From our friends closer to us, we can receive a more intimate gift. We can receive a voice. With that voice we can return again to the world with something to give and something to say. Earlham College professor Paul Lacey raised my awareness of this process, drawing it from the authors of *Women's Ways of Knowing*: "Unlike the eye, the ear requires closeness between subject and object. Unlike seeing, speaking and listening suggest dialogue and interaction."[11]

Coming to Voice

Here's a story from my own journey of coming to voice. It illustrates the movement from silence to voice several times as well as the connection between our incarnational Anabaptist model and the Enlightenment-based models in the academy around us. In 1987 I attended a Wingspread Conference on Service Learning among the founders of Campus Compact.

I listened to these high-minded and good-hearted leaders speak about how important community service is and yet how hard it is to reward faculty and students for engaging in it. I could not relate my own experience at all to what they were saying. Then I had one of those "bell" moments. "They are trying to graft back onto their institutions what was separated by the epistemology they espouse," I thought. "When science and religion, head and heart, and theory and application split, these institutions created hierarchies that perpetually privilege one side of the split over the other. Only a religious world view – another epistemology – one that disappeared, if it ever existed, from their campuses decades or centuries ago, will support service as much as it supports scholarship." I was not bold enough to speak my thoughts, however. I sat in silence a long while as other people talked.

At some point in that conversation, I found myself on my feet, telling a story. I told them service has to be a way of life to be meaningful. It has to have a connection to the very reason people teach and do research. To be meaningful and non-exploitative, service has to have intrinsic reward. Then I described the first-year general education reading and writing course I was teaching, and my student, "Jeff." Jeff had written in his journal that he could not write about the role of silence in Chaim Potok's *The Chosen* as I had requested. But, he said, if you read between the lines, you might understand. During my individual interview with Jeff, I told him I wanted to read between the lines. I wanted to know what he knew about silence. Slowly, he told me the story of how he had lost his father in a boating accident while the family had been on vacation 11 years earlier. And how at age seven he had become "the man of the family." Where his father's voice had been, there was silence. He had not recognized the depth of his loss until he read about the silence between Reb Saunders and his son Reuven in *The Chosen*. He said he had never cried for his father. And as he said those words, tears began to flow. They flowed until they were sobs. And I cried with him. I told him that the silence he had endured was creating in him a compassionate heart, and that having such a heart was what all true learning is all about.

Such life-altering encounters, I suspect, are not unusual at church-related colleges. When I told that story at Wingspread, there was complete silence in the room. I did not know, do not know to this day, how much of it was scorn and how much of it was stunned confusion, but I think it was the silence that occurs after a bell has been struck.

My first point, then, is that we must pay attention to the signs of our time. The newfound interest of the "secular" world in things we consider sacred is fascinating. Such an interest behooves us to examine what we do, to be self-critical, and then to be willing to offer our understandings to the world at large. Words like "wisdom," "soul," "spirit," "service," – words that were anathema or simply archaic a decade ago – are now popping up everywhere. They are fads, but they are also calls for help from our culture. If those of us in higher education live our personal and institutional missions with integrity, we can expect to be called out of our silence into speech.

Transforming Experiences

Where can we go for instruction in integrity, truth-telling, and trans-formation from silence into speech? We can go to all the liberating arts and sciences. For a Goshen College model, I would not focus on the triangle of learning, faith, and life described by those at, for instance, Wheaton College.[12] In fact, I would not use a triangle at all. I would choose a circle. It could be a Venn diagram with each of those areas having its own circle and its own intersection with every other circle and a place in the center where they all meet. Or it could be a single circle that functions like a wheel, with rounded arrows on the outside, showing movement from faith to learning to life and back again around the wheel. The pedagogy we use in the Study-Service Term (SST) is action-reflection-response. This pedagogy has found a home at Goshen College because it first had a home – an unnamed home – in our experience as Mennonites and because it has a larger home in learning theory.

Our students at Goshen College are mostly white, mostly middle-class. Yet if the dormitory walls were to give up their secrets, they would ring with stories of suffering and ecstasy that come from such places as Chengdu, Abidjan, Jakarta, Port au Prince, San Jose, Tegucigalpa, Jena, Santo Domingo, and hundreds of villages from all parts of the globe. Students make meaning out of experiences such as watching a sleek Mercedes with tinted windows roar past beggars lined up on both sides of the street, walking through suffocatingly beautiful rain forests, digging wells, worshipping in mud huts – or in a spectacular basilica surrounded by hovels – trying to understand the mysterious opposite sex under even more mysterious circumstances, recognizing the privilege Americans carry with their passports and the resentment privilege breeds. The most touching stories, however, usually come from the families with whom students live and the generosity of their hospitality. Students return home with softer, more sensitive, hearts and stronger minds. If a student reads about some cultural fact first and then sees a version of the practice or value described, there is either an "aha" moment – a "bell" moment – or a moment of cognitive dissonance due to either the perception or the reality differing from the expected. Even people who want to be objective or detached cannot avoid the subjective on SST. But those who gravitate to the subjective are not safe either. If they are to make meaning, they must draw back far enough to see and seek information outside themselves. They are not "integrating" faith and learning, learning and life, faith and life on SST. Faith *is* learning *is* life.

The narratives of SST, though different in every case, often bear the mark of the redemption narratives of the Bible, whether or not our students – and even faculty – always recognize these marks. Listen to these words from student David Roth, writing after returning to his SST location in Dominican Republic following four days in Haiti:

> Going to bed tonight tired, but a good tired that has come from thoroughly extending myself in every intellectual, emotional and physical way during the Haiti trip. I am spent intellectually – I pushed so hard to soak up every word from every speaker, pushed my brain constantly for three days, examining/connecting/critiquing ideas presented to me. I spent myself in staying up late all the nights to talk among wonderful people in fascinating subject areas. And I've never learned so much in three days, never. I think my life/views/opinions have been altered permanently in some areas, like thinking about poverty, and about dependence/service issues, and about entering a culture you have little knowledge of. And it feels good to be spent. The rush I got from all the input has given me so much to ponder in a long-term sense.[13]

Both the deliberate placement of the student in a disorienting situation and assigning him to learn via the reflective mode of journaling are part of the pedagogy and part of the deeply imbedded and sometimes silent philosophical-theological structure of our curriculum. The form the student gravitates toward naturally is the narrative. From silence and struggle comes story. Stories and hymns have seen us through for about 500 years. Perhaps, ironically, one reason why we have not explained our narratives philosophically or theologically is that we have experienced their reality so profoundly and find them to be self-evident, requiring little or no justification.

However, the purpose of examining David's journal is to observe the structure of his narrative and some of the allusions to the biblical narrative one could draw out of it. Robert Frost has said that poetry begins in wonder and ends in wisdom. In this case, the narrator begins in exhaustion and ends in a "rush" that he recognizes will be the stock-pile of memory on which he will draw – "ponder" – for the rest of his life. If I were writing comments on this entry, something the faculty leaders do on SST, I would point out to David that he has written in these sentences his own psalm, with a typical structure of great exertion mixed with pain leading to deep satisfaction from yielded-ness. He could even read about the role of disorientation and reorientation by reading theologian Walter Brueggemann's book *The Message of the Psalms*.[14] He has therefore discovered something profound about his own name, "David." He has also wrestled, like Jacob, for a blessing. Now, like Mary, he will ponder these things in his heart.

I do not consider such observations to be "mere piety" – a patina of religiosity over an experience not presented as explicitly religious by the student. Rather, I see this as an opportunity simultaneously to deepen learning (has David ever thought about the structure of the Psalms?) and deepen faith (does he recognize the biblical power of naming for his own calling in life?).

Naming Our Students

The author Madeleine L'Engle has visited the Goshen campus at least three times during my years at the college. I have read her trilogy to both my children. Inside a dog-eared copy of her book *The Wind and the Door* is her admonition, in her own handwriting, to my son, Anthony, penned 17 years ago: "Be a namer." Ever since L'Engle named the process of naming for me, and ever since I read the passage in that same book about Progo the angel, whose job it is to name all the stars, I have had a deep appreciation for the power of naming in education, especially church-related education. What would happen to the world if every one of our students left our campuses truly and deeply named? L'Engle herself would say that war and violence would subside and the world would reflect more clearly God's design in creation. The secret to building a redemptive community is to lavish love and attention on each of its members, as God has lavished love on us. What could be a more profound way of doing that than helping each member discover meaning in his or her name? We become peacemakers as we ourselves are filled with the peace that passes understanding. We become servants as we are served by Christ upon his knees.

When each member of a community comes to know the meaning of his or her own name, another kind of naming occurs – the naming of the evil powers and principalities – that attempt to separate us from the love of God. As we become firmly rooted ourselves, our eyes open to the rootlessness around us. Theologians John Howard Yoder and Walter Wink have expounded on the concept and redeemed it for a secular age.[15] Walter Wink has also suggested that institutions, as well as individuals, can draw sustenance from the idea of vocation. Wink notes that in the book of Revelation the New Testament churches of various cities were addressed not by the name of their cities, but by the names of the Angels who defend the church from the Powers and Principalities, then asks us to consider the possibility of taking seriously what kind of angels our institutions might have or recover.[16]

The path from silence to voice often passes through suffering. And often the path is fraught with conflict. Therefore it is great territory for artists. The flourishing of the arts among us is a sign that we are ready to come to voice. Among two highlights on campus in one recent year was a conference on Mennonites Writing in the U.S., which attracted 300 people, and the production of *Preacher/Poet*[17] by our drama department. In *Preacher/Poet*, excerpts from multiple Mennonite theologians, church leaders, novelists, and artists were woven together into a powerful performance. I would like to use a selection from the novel *The Salvation of Yasch Siemens* to test the thesis that the arts can instruct us as we move from silence to voice.

I am almost completely ignorant of the Canadian Mennonite community the writer Armin Wiebe uses for his base in this novel. But it does not matter. For I recognized myself and my people even if I do not know "flat German" or the Russian place names in the book. And I imagine that others who are not Mennonite could recognize something they know in this narrative also. Here is a work of fiction, turned into drama, that involves music, and, when it was in full production here, included paintings on silk, highlighted by spotlights on both sides of the stage. We see the arts emerge in this story as they have emerged in our church. We see that they tell a tale of conflict, caricatured in the images of the pope, the czar, and the Brunk revivalist. Music, the "Ode to Joy," no less, resolves not only this conflict, but the conflict of what will happen to the rebellious boys who skipped church. And behind all this sensory carnival beats the drum, a reminder, to me at least, of the narrative of creation under the narrative of salvation and incarnation. Listen to Armin Wiebe's words. Listen "between the lines." Think about how the underlying beat, like the hidden wholeness of creation, helps bring Hova Jake to voice:

> The brummtupp plays real quiet, like it's getting the beat ready for a song, and even in the barn when Hova was practicing it didn't sound like that. It still reaches something deep inside the blood but it's not so simple, it's almost like some music I heard on CFAM once with my crystal radio and I couldn't get any other station and then Hova Jake begins to sing: "Joyful, joyful, we adore thee, God of Glory, Lord of Love."[18]

In his chapter in the *Models for Christian Higher Education* text, Rod Sawatsky says we need a theology of creation. We undoubtedly do. But we undoubtedly already have such a theology in a work of art like this one, also. Our colleges must continue to be the place in the church where the arts can flourish, where they can help us with our own need for continuities of conflict as well as doxological celebration.[19]

Making New Connections

The arts provide one potential avenue for the kind of passionate spirituality that Episcopal priest Loren Mead calls for in his book *Five*

Challenges for the Once and Future Church.[20] But if Anabaptist education is to fulfill its promise in the 21st century, it also will need to make new connections to missions and to worship. We need more people of color in our classrooms and in our administrations. We will need to go where the church is. We need to share the contemporary word of mission and not just the historical word of tradition. Without such grounding, we too will lose the root connection to service and to spirituality in our curriculum that is so observable in the research university and in the secular liberal arts college. We will have found our voice only to lose it again.

There is a meaningful task for all of us in every institution. We need to address pedagogy, theology, philosophy, history, the arts, the sciences. We need to examine the medieval and contemplative side of Anabaptism – where silence was a blessing and not a curse. We need to write and speak and find ways to manage the multiplicity of voices as they arise. Therefore we need even more emphasis on peacemaking. And on the active training of peacemakers in every setting; starting with the home and church would be a good idea, I think.

I will end with one more story, that of colonial schoolmaster Christopher Dock, whose name we have invoked often in Mennonite higher education and yet whose voice has been largely lost to us. He was far ahead of his age, not only in the fact that he did not use the rod for discipline but also in his use of music and rewards given by both teacher and parents. But we know very few biographical facts about him. We have some stories, most of which are hard to document. And we have his remarkable book, *Schulordnung.* In reading through this book, which is so filled with silences and Dock's grave and deeply pious doubts about whether he ought to write it at all, I found an example of a namer *par excellence.* His starting point is that teaching is a divine calling. His method is love, like that of the shepherd for the sheep. His practice is prayer. The Bible was his primer and his graduate course. And his uses of it suggest a deep understanding of the Inner Teacher. Listen to this passage: "When the pupils have had much practice in finding references, they are at times put to the test and reminded that outward seeking is not in itself undesirable, but that it should be tried in another form. I let them sit very still, pay attention, and think no idle thoughts, but the first passage that enters their minds, they shall stand and read. In this exercise I have often marveled how God 'has perfected praise out of the mouths of babes and sucklings' ...."[21]

Oliver Wendell Schenk's famous painting of Dock shows him kneeling in his schoolroom with the list of his students' names in his hand. One story, repeated often, has it that he died in such a posture, praying for his students by name. He had been lifted and struck as a bell often throughout his life. His writing echoes with the sound of that call. The last time he was struck, he lifted. I cannot imagine a better death – or a better life.

---

1. Shirley Hershey Showalter is President of Goshen College. This essay is adapted from a presentation at the Imagination and Reflections for Church-Related Higher Education: Models Meaningful for Mennonites conference, Goshen College, 18 April 1998.

2. Annie Dillard, *Pilgrim at Tinker Creek* (New York: Harper & Row, 1985).

3. Bender's vision, originally an address at the American Society of Church History, December 1943, first appeared in *Church History* 13 (March 1944), 3-24, and *The Mennonite Quarterly Review* 18 (April 1944), 67-88. It has been reprinted repeatedly since that time.

4. Richard T. Hughes and William B. Adrian, eds., *Models for Christian Higher Education: Strategies for Success in the Twenty-First Century* (Grand Rapids: William B. Eerdmans, 1997). The Schlabach essay in this volume is adapted from his chapter in the *Models* text. Rodney J. Sawatsky is president of Messiah College and former president of Conrad Grebel College. Paul Toews is professor of history at Fresno Pacific College and director of the Center for Mennonite Brethren Studies, Fresno Pacific College and Mennonite Brethren Biblical Seminary.

5. Rodney J. Sawatsky, "What Can the Mennonite Tradition Contribute to Christian Higher Education," in Hughes and Adrian, *Models for Christian Higher Education*, 192. The James C. Juhnke quote is from his *Vision, Doctrines, War: Mennonite Identity and Organizations in America, 1890-1930* (Scottdale: Herald Press, 1989), 165.

6. See Schlabach's essay titled "Goshen College and Its Church Relations: History and Reflections" in this volume.

7. Paul Toews, "Religious Idealism and Academic Vocation at Fresno Pacific College," in Hughes and Adrian, *Models for Christian Higher Education*, 226.

8. See the essay by Keith Graber Miller in this volume for a synopsis of Sawatsky's notion of incarnation in relation to Mennonite higher education. Wilbur Birky's essay in this volume also draws on incarnational language.

9. Paul Toews, "Religious Idealism," 228.

10. See James Woodress, *Willa Cather: A Literary Life* (Lincoln: University of Nebraska Press, 1989).

11. Mary Field Belenky, Blythe McVicker Clinchy, Nancy Rule Goldberger,

Jill Mattuck Tarule, *Women's Way of Knowing: The Development of Self, Voice, and Mind* (New York: Basic Books, 1986), 18.

12. Taken from a presentation by Arthur Holmes of Wheaton College at the Imagination and Reflections for Church Related Higher Education: Models Meaningful for Mennonites conference, 17 April 1998.

13. The quote, used with Roth's permission, is taken from a Dean's Workshop presentation by SST leader Keith Graber Miller, August 1997. See also Graber Miller, "A One-Armed Embrace of Postmodernity: International Education and Church-Related Colleges," in Stephen Haynes and Corrie Norman, *Talking Out of Place: Professing in the Postmodern Academy* (Waco: Baylor University Press, forthcoming).

14. Brueggemann describes the Psalms as being roughly organized into three general themes: poems of *orientation* (songs of guaranteed creation), poems of *disorientation* (songs of disarray), and poems of *new orientation* (songs of surprising new life). The Psalms' expressions of a faithful life are characterized by decisive movements toward new orientation. See Walter Brueggemann, *The Message of the Psalms: A Theological Commentary* (Minneapolis: Augsburg, 1984), 19-21.

15. See, e.g., John Howard Yoder, *The Politics of Jesus*, 2nd edition (Grand Rapids: William B. Eerdmans,1994), and Walter Wink, *Engaging the Powers: Discernment and Resistance in a World of Domination* (Minneapolis: Fortress Press, 1992).

16. See especially chapter 16 in Wink's *Engaging the Powers*.

17. *Preacher/Poet* was compiled by Doug Liechty Caskey, Beth Martin Birky, and Billie Jean Wiebe from various Mennonites' published works.

18. Armin Wiebe, *The Salvation of Yasch Siemens* (Winnipeg: Turnstone, 1984), 28-29.

19. The phrase "continuities of conflict" is from Paul Lacey and the term "doxological celebration" is from Arthur Holmes in their presentations at the Imagination and Reflections for Church-Related Higher Education: Models Meaningful for Mennonites conference, 17-18 April 1998.

20. Loren Mead, *Five Challenges for the Once and Future Church* (Washington: Alban Institute, 1991).

21. Christopher Dock, *Excerpts from* Schulordnung (School Management) and *Selections from* A Hundred Necessary Rules of Conduct for Children, Martin G. Burmbaugh, trans. (Harrisonburg: Association of Elementary Schools, 1908), 9. See also John D. Martin, *Christopher Dock: Pioneer Christian Schoolmaster on the Skippack* (Harrisonburg: Christian Light, 1971) and Gerald C. Studer, *Christopher Dock, Colonial Schoolmaster: The Biography and Writings of Christopher Dock* (Scottdale: Herald Press, 1967).

4

A LIBERAL ARTS VISION

Paul A. Keim[1]

The General Education curriculum is not an end in itself, but is an instrument, or strategy, or method whereby the salient features of the liberal arts philosophy of higher education are made available to our students. At the heart of this philosophy is an idea, an aggressive assertion, an *a priori* commitment, that only an educated person, that is, one who is aware of self and of the other, one capable of independent discernment, analysis, and judgment, one open to testing and being tested by the Unknown, one gripped by an insatiable quest for truth, can be truly free.

Our mission statement begins with the assertion that Goshen College is a four-year liberal arts college "dedicated to the development of informed, articulate, sensitive, responsible Christians." It is our belief that education, training, and socialization into the liberal arts tradition are at the very heart of everything we do at Goshen College. All disciplines, programs, departments, major and minor fields of study, practical experiences, activities, and initiatives must be measured against this primary commitment. Whatever falls short of, or detracts us from, this fundamental commitment must be removed, replaced, renewed, or transformed.

To say that at the heart of the liberal arts philosophy of higher education is an idea, a spirit, a timeless constant, is to concede that it cannot ultimately be contained in structures. We must accept constant refinement of the idea and constant transformations of the structures, which give it expression as a normal, necessary condition of its vitality and effectiveness.

Pursuing the Truth

Furthermore, the pursuit of truth and beauty, the commitment of a life of learning, is a self-legitimizing activity. It is an idea that need serve no particular ideology or creed. According to Genesis, the Creation in all its aspects is in and of itself a moral good (1:31). Truth is the goal and the path. Truth is the only acceptable criterion for judging the Good, for only the truth can truly liberate. "And you shall know the truth, and the truth shall set you free" (John 8:32).

"And what is truth?" Pilate asked (John 18:38). It is a good question and does not, in my view, reflect negatively on Pilate's character. There are different perspectives on truth, and even different, competing, and perhaps even mutually exclusive truths, even in the Bible. So where does that leave us? It leaves us no better nor worse than the undeniable fact of our mortality leaves us. We might wish it were not so – but it is, and shall remain. The consciousness of this reality produces all the tension and conflict and resolution and redemption which we know of as culture. It is no different with the unsettling reality that we inhabit subjective, constructed worlds – in conversation with but never completely coterminous with the worlds of our friends or our enemies.

At its best, the liberal arts tradition in a Christian context is characterized by a greater, not lesser commitment to the liberation that proceeds from the pursuit of truth. It should accept fewer, not more, restraints in the quest for the knowledge of beauty and virtue. It should provide a framework of faith that liberates the individual from the fears and limitations inherent in the human consciousness of mortality. It should model a liberation which affirms acceptance of self, makes commitment to others possible, lifts the principle of loving the neighbor, the Other, even one's enemy to a normative standard of human behavior, and celebrates life in all facets of its awesome mystery. Liberal arts in a Christian context should enable us to live more fully "as if." We live *as if* we will never die; we live *as if* we can trust others; we live *as if* there were order and meaning and purpose in the universe, in nature and culture. And somehow this "as if" enhances and enriches our lives, as individuals and communities; allows us to love and be loved; allows us to find hope in the midst of suffering; allows us to shake our fists at the heavens and cry into the tempest; gives us courage to take the consequences, to flirt with immortality, and to die with dignity.

Learning Together

In an educational community committed to the liberal arts, all learn together. No one ceases to learn, develop, and grow. All are encouraged to make forays out of their comfort zones, into the world of the Other. No one person or group of people has exclusive claims to truth. Knowledge, experience, insight, wisdom, erudition, articulate expression, proficiency, achievement – all these are valued characteristics. The gifts and intelligences of each individual are valued, encouraged, and celebrated.

The pursuit of truth in the Christian liberal arts tradition is a path of peace and must reject any action that threatens, devalues, or destroys human life or degrades our ecological home. It affirms life in all its aspects, accepts mortality as a natural part of life, and believes in a reality stronger than death.

The faculty in a liberal arts institution are full members of a noble profession, but they also have a special calling. They must be equipped to address the challenges and issues of the human condition beyond the narrow confines of their particular tradition and the exclusivity of their specialized training. They need to be concerned with and committed to the total well-being of their students, learning as they teach, sharing their wisdom, listening, mentoring, always ready to be transformed by new insights, reinvigorated by ongoing study, nurtured by the interlocking communities of which they are members. They need the time and resources to think as well as teach, to write and produce as well as lecture, to debate and discuss as well as grade.

Anyone not committed to this fundamental vision, this primary mission of the college should be invited to seek gainful employment elsewhere.

We must begin to ask ourselves how to educate our students, not in ways that simply correspond to our training, but as part of an educational community which prepares students for the world they will fully encounter when they graduate. This will draw deeply on our professional knowledge and experience, but even more so on our character. We must cultivate an environment of learning which holds in creative tension the experiential and practical as well as the theoretical and abstract. The modeling we do for students will have increased significance in this regard. We are to represent and personify lives devoted to scholarship, and to culture for service.

Entering the World

What is the kind of world our students will be entering as graduates? It is a multicultural and multilingual world. It can be competitive and depersonalizing. It is a world empowered and depersonalized by technology, where computer and communication skills are prerequisites for survival rather than enhancements of privilege. It is a world of almost unlimited information in the context of which the ability to make discriminating choices about meaning will separate managers from laborers, leaders from followers, those with a voice in the determination of their own destiny from those who have few choices. It is a world that flings the sons and daughters of traditional communities into a mobile labor market as isolated souls. It cares less for the have-nots, allows higher concentrations of wealth in the hands of fewer of its citizens, allows more families to slip beneath the poverty line, is quicker to use military force to solve its problems, and uses religion to legitimate its grip on privilege.

What will our students need to meet the challenges of such a world – to live and work in the world? To thrive in the world? To compete in the world? To speak to the world? To transform the world? To become responsible citizens of the world? Our specific answers to these questions will surely change over time. But our underlying commitment remains: to provide an education that promotes and affirms the wisdom of head and heart, nurtures mature faith, is uncompromising in the pursuit of excellence, and models lives of service. It is our conviction that such an education will remain a pearl of great price.

---

1. Paul A. Keim is Vice President for Academic Affairs and Academic Dean at Goshen College. This essay is from a previously unpublished piece circulated with General Education revision materials, 1998.

5

THE VISION, HISTORY, AND ETHOS OF GOSHEN COLLEGE'S STUDY-SERVICE TERM

Wilbur J. Birky[1]

Goshen College's Study-Service Term didn't just happen. It is rooted in our theology of service, in the Mennonite Church's practice of service abroad during World War II, in a key observation of an accreditation team in the mid-1960s, in President Paul Mininger's appointment of The Committee on the Future of the College in 1965, and in Henry Weaver's shepherding of the faculty toward an innovative decision in 1966-67. Three pilot units went to Barbados, Haiti, and Colombia in the summer of 1967; the full-fledged SST program began in 1968, and has continued ever since.

Now, some 32 years later, over 6,200 students have gone on SST, and more than 125 Goshen teaching and administrative faculty have served as SST leaders, along with their spouses or assistants. More than 50 of these are still on the faculty. Goshen's SST units have operated in 16 separate countries: five in Central America, four in the Caribbean, three in Asia, two in eastern Europe, and two in west Africa.

A Theology of Service

In an April 27, 1989 address to a Wingspread Conference on International Education and Service Learning, former GC President J. Lawrence Burkholder suggested that international education and service had become an "article of faith" for Goshen College. He further articulated our vision for international education as "oriented in service, backed by a philosophy or theology of service to the neighbor, administered by a caring faculty and approved by parents and freely chosen by students."[2] Former President Paul Mininger cited SST as a program under which "students would not just observe human need, but that they would also act to meet some of those needs. We wanted students to take action on behalf of other persons, an action that would have moral consequences."[3]

This concept of service has been built into SST from the beginning, not only in the "study-service" name but also into the very structure of our program where six of our thirteen weeks are spent in active work assignments alongside nationals. All SST leaders, and we hope most SST students, have become aware that achieving "service" in any truly "productive" sense in six weeks is somewhat dubious. But the very tension created by this ambiguity, and the necessary discussions about it, have served a creative purpose in the practice of what we have come to call "service-learning."

A Metaphor of Incarnation

Among the many Biblical metaphors which may enrich our understanding of the vision for SST is that of the Incarnation. Let us propose the Incarnation as an act of divine imagination rooted in a profound realization that even God could not *know and understand* the human condition completely without *entering into* it, to experience it in the body. That was a true cross-cultural experience. So a description of at least the early parts of Jesus' incarnation applies aptly to the SST experience: it is to give up one's customary place of comfort, to become as a child, to learn a new language, to eat in new ways, to be received into a new family, to work in the mundane "carpentry shop," to attend the local house of worship, to question and be questioned, to experience frustration and success, and to

62

learn to serve in the very "thick" of life. This is service-learning in the context of *crossing over* into the life of the "other." If necessary for God, how much more so for us is this knowledge by experience for compassionate action.

A History: Ethos as Educational Destiny?

World War II and its aftermath provided something of an "incarnational" training ground for a crucial concentration of GC faculty who were to help adopt SST and lead some of its first-generation programs. In "Faculty Experience Factor in SST Origin," former President Victor Stoltzfus lists at least 24 GC faculty members (plus spouses) who served in at least 13 countries spread over four continents during the 1940s and 1950s – many with Mennonite Central Committee in various forms of reconstruction and education in the years following World War II.[4]

But also in these impressive numbers lay the basis of a startlingly simple observation in the 1965 North Central Association of Schools and Colleges' accreditation report. As reported by Henry D. Weaver, who justifiably came to be known as the "father of SST," the NCA team "pointed out that we had an unusual resource in the 50 percent of the faculty who had lived abroad; however…that we were not making use of this expertise in any special way."[5] It is as if the obvious facts of our collective faculty experience stood suddenly as an expression of both our historical ethos and our educational destiny. President Paul Mininger's Committee on the Future of the College fairly quickly reached consensus on directions for a new program, Assistant to the President Henry Weaver developed the basic design and led the faculty in open debate, and by the fall of 1968 the Study-Service Term was in full swing as the preferred option for a new international education requirement.

A Paradigm for Transformative Education in Community

Our vision as an institution and for the SST program is rightly focused on students. But returning SST leaders frequently credit SST for significant growth in their own practice of teaching. Ruth Krall, SST leader and past International Education Committee chair, describes her own "conversion" as a teacher:

Previously my conception of teaching and learning was that the teacher was responsible to be strong, not weak; to be informed, not confused; to be loving and perceptive of students, not needful of love and perceptivity.... But in Costa Rica, I was not an expert. I was not always strong. I was not always loving and culturally perceptive.... Honesty about painful feelings and confusion did not appear to destroy [students'] inner security nor did it seem to cause a lack of trust. Walking the same road as they did each day made us into co-learners.... One enduring result of SST in my personal life has been this basic challenge to my theories of teaching and learning. I am more committed to relational teaching.[6]

Few former SST leaders speak of the experience as easy; most speak of it as exhausting but highly rewarding in holistic and sometimes transformative ways. On the whole, our strongest advocates of the SST program are its former leaders. As an institution we have formalized this commitment in our ten learning outcomes, four of which serve as significant guides for SST programming. These four are the ones which call for an active development of "intercultural openness," of "the ability to communicate in a variety of sign systems," of "action-reflection learning," and of "a healthy understanding of self and others."

Still another manifestation of SST's appeal to holistic learning is the fact that, over the years, we have drawn very effective leadership from both academic and administrative "sides" of the faculty. In its advisory role, International Education Committee members have not always agreed on formal qualifications for SST leader selection. But it is clear that correlation between effective SST leadership and an openness to learning holistic modes of teaching is much higher than the correlation between effectiveness and one's identity as a professor or administrator. Most SST leaders from both groups have grown significantly in their sense of educational mission through this powerful experience.

Norman Kauffmann, Dean of Students for 28 years and Goshen's primary researcher on the impact of SST on students, suggests that our

SST program is a worthy educational paradigm for all of our teaching. "SST represents this new educational model," he writes. "The students who experience SST as it is meant to be are more than superficially involved in another culture and cannot separate academic learning from personal growth." Kauffmann insists that this new knowledge and this changed worldview "cannot be held at arm's length, divorced from their personal lives. Immersion will not permit students to be only spectators in the world in which they live."[7]

Goshen's current president, Shirley Hershey Showalter, sounds the appropriate note for the continuing vision not only of our SST program, but also for applying its lessons at home. In accepting her call to the presidency, she said:

> We have seen today that our past is a rich one and that we are well positioned for the next millennium if we simultaneously build upon and expand our base.... We will develop what African-American scholar Henry Louis Gates, Jr. calls "a rigorous multiculturalism," building on what we have learned from the Study-Service Term abroad and bringing it back home with us so that we can face such evils as racism and sexism and violence courageously. We will do such things not because they are, in that awful phrase, "politically correct," but because they are right.[8]

And so with a powerful vision rooted in our history, our commitments, our ethos, and more than 30 years of SST experience, we hope to keep service-learning alive both abroad and at home.

---

1. Wilbur J. Birky, a former Professor of English, is Director of International Education at Goshen College. This essay is adapted from *2000-01 SST Faculty Handbook*, Goshen College.

2. J. Lawrence Burkholder, "The Idea of Service in International Education," in Stuart W. Showalter, ed., *The Role of Service-Learning in International Education: Proceedings of a Wingspread Conference, held April 26-28, 1989, at Racine, Wisconsin* (Goshen: Goshen College, 1989), 29.

3. Paul Mininger, "A Radical Vision for International Education," *Goshen College Bulletin* 73.4 (July 1988), 24.

4. Victor Stoltzfus, "Faculty Experience Factor in SST Origin," *Goshen College Bulletin* 73.6 (November 1988), 24.

5. Henry D. Weaver, "The Goshen Faculty Create SST," *Goshen College Bulletin* 73.4 (July 1988), 2-3.

6. Ruth Krall, "Leading SST Convinces Krall Relational Teaching is Best," *Goshen College Bulletin* 73.6 (November 1988), 5.

7. Norman Kauffmann, "Impact on Students Varies, Depending on Maturity, Immersion," *Goshen College Bulletin* 74.1 (January 1989), 4.

8. Shirley Hershey Showalter, unpublished acceptance speech, 29 April 1996.

6

TEACHING AND LEARNING
AS FAITHFUL DISCIPLESHIP

Kathy Meyer Reimer and Scott Barge[1]

What is *Mennonite* about teaching and learning at Goshen College?
Many of the elements of education at Goshen College are likely
common to other small, private liberal arts colleges. And yet,
through conversation with others in the higher-education world,
there does seem to be something unique about the way we do our
educating at GC. What does it mean to *choose* to place oneself in a
context with others who also want to be at a Mennonite college?
What happens when we bring to the fore both our like-mindedness
and our diversity? Does this context bring out elements not necessarily present at other small schools? As a professor and a student
who chose to be a part of Goshen College, we have asked ourselves
just why we made this choice, what effect the choice has had on us,
and whether some of the issues we think about are unique to
Mennonite higher education. We are conducting part of this conversation on paper with the hope that others may join in.

   *Looking back on my (Scott's) four years of Mennonite higher
education, I realize the path I followed has been determined by
default as much as by intentional choice. Growing up in the
Mennonite church essentially guided me – with little resistance on
my part – to the doors of the Mennonite colleges. Ironically, my*

rationale for coming to Goshen four years ago only minimally coin-cides with what I hold to be most dear about this experience in ret-rospect. The unique aspects of Goshen College and its people have, instead, been slowly revealed to me – whispered in my ear – as I have gone about living in the campus community.

From the beginning, I expected to be surrounded by some people who hold beliefs similar to mine. Coming from a public high school, this was a refreshing and welcomed change. I suddenly was able to talk with others about a common experience and draw upon the commonality as I worked to better define myself. From the outset, I also anticipated form-ing the relationships possible in a smaller educational environment. My high school was a small one, and I looked forward to the same in my col-lege experience. Indeed, both of these expectations were met, and exceeded.

I (Kathy) graduated from Goshen College, taught elementary school for a number of years, and then went to graduate school for further study in pedagogy and literacy. It was in the teaching world and graduate school that I first came to see how different my Goshen College educa-tion had been from the experiences of some of my peers. I also came to a greater awareness of the roots of some of the pedagogical and institu-tional differences I was encountering. I returned to Goshen College nine years ago after working at a large research university. I had intended to accept a position at another research university, but received a call about an opening at GC. After conversations with GC professors and adminis-trators, we decided to move to Goshen instead. In doing so, I realized that not only did I see a very different life as a faculty member at Goshen College, but I also held GC to a different standard than I held my former universities. What were and continue to be the different expectations to which I hold Goshen College?

I expect a different kind of relationship with students – one that includes a kind of extended contact and interaction that is difficult at a larger institution. I expect a different kind of interaction with administrators – one of shared goals, mutual respect, listening, and some stake in decision-making. I expect different emphases to guide my curriculum and my research. I expect a different academic, per-sonal, and spiritual experience – one that integrates all three areas and that also is consistent across all three areas. Particularly for a Mennonite college, I expect those who preach peace to practice it in their personal and institutional lives – which means I assume a different kind of interaction and way to deal with the conflict that naturally arises in any growing and dynamic institution.

Some of these distinctions could happen at any small liberal arts college. Professors elsewhere use much of what I do methodologically or instructionally. The kinds of relationships and interactions I have with students could happen at some other colleges or universities as well. However, the content of my interactions and the context for my interactions are, in many ways, unique to Goshen College.

Distinctions in Content

One sort of content is the curriculum we offer at GC. While our courses are firmly rooted in current theory and research, we also have an unusually high number of classes with "real life experiences" attached – for example, practica. But it is not always courses *within* any one field that distinguish our students as much as the other courses and involvements they bring to a given discipline.

I have been able to participate in many areas that are not directly related to my field, teacher education. This has meant being able to take Bible and religion, peace studies, and TESOL (Teaching English as a Second Language) classes, living and studying abroad for a semester, and participating in music lessons and ensembles. In each of these areas, what began as casual interests has grown into understandings that are key to how I approach my major. Connections between Bible, religion, peace studies and TESOL form a web "under the surface" which spans all of the content areas. The further I advanced into the study of teaching, the more I was able to pinpoint my goals for my classrooms. Interestingly, though, these goals were influenced as much by the other courses I was taking as they were by my pedagogy courses.

As I came to better understand the life of Jesus, I began to see themes I wanted to bring into my teaching – even in a secular public-school setting. In my classroom, how we approach life together can, without direct religious content, model for students the peaceable, communal life to which Jesus calls us. How we approach the diversity present in the room, how we talk about needs and wants in the context of the greater world, and, perhaps most importantly, how we address conflict and violence can all influence the lenses through which my students view the world and how they interact with it. Two semesters of peace studies courses greatly influenced where I stand on these issues, but so, too, did teaching in diverse schools 20 minutes away in Elkhart, studying literature of spiritual reflection and social action, and living abroad during the Study-Service Term (SST).

Many of my students have a good deal of expertise in conflict transformation or peace studies. Many students have TESOL or Intercultural Studies minors. All of these are cutting-edge programs at universities and in the work place, but Goshen College offered them long before they were in vogue. TESOL, Study-Service Term, intercultural studies, and peace, justice and conflict studies, I would suggest, are closely related to Goshen's Mennonite education. Having facility in crossing cultures is not just a leg up in the business world. If we are to truly work for peace we must understand others. If we are evangelical and mission-minded, we must know how to meet others in their own cultures and places. If we want to speak for justice and advocate for those who are marginalized, it is essential to experience some marginalization ourselves or at least to place ourselves in contexts where we live with, interact with, and study with those who are marginalized. How can we hold these concepts as a faith community if we don't provide for the study, critical analysis, and integration that will allow students to make it a part of their own faith? That is why it is important to offer the breadth of educational options that we do.

Pulling together the many aspects of a truly liberal arts education is, I believe, tied to what might be termed Mennonite "practical idealism." One might describe Mennonite theology as "living in the now of the not yet" – meaning that we feel we can and should act in the world on the basis of our beliefs. This means living in a way which models our understanding of what it means to be disciples, believing that we can be agents of social change. Our faith is not one sequestered in the personal or spiritual realm – it is one that is active and visible in how we live our daily lives.

Teaching is a concrete, tangible acting out of my faith, and these aspects are critical to my faith and, I would hope, to the faith of my students. Each term students fill out an evaluation form about professors. Two of the statements students are asked to respond to are "Professor gave attention to concerns of the Christian faith" and

"Course helped me relate faith and knowledge in this field." What a victory it is when students respond that such integration happened for them in a course. For it is because of our faith that we talk about access to education, poverty, those who do not fit our schools as we have them organized, parents, neighborhoods, and diversity. We discuss these issues not only because educators face them, but also because they are faith issues. Who we are, how we teach, how we relate to students, and how we shape our curriculum is a statement of our faith, commitments, and beliefs. My teaching is how I live out my faith.

This explains much about why I am able to find such inter-relatedness "under the surface." After a few semesters I realized that many faculty members and administrators at Goshen believe their roles at the college are intertwined with living out their faith. My education has drawn together previously compartmentalized areas of my life – faith and work. It seems to me that for many professors at Goshen College teaching is faithful discipleship. This act of educating is part of a larger picture. Faculty members are investing themselves in an institution and mission that strives not merely to further the membership of the academy, but to shape people who will become vital, contributing members of the church. In this sense, faculty are engaged in service to the church and to the larger global community. As a student, then, I am on the receiving end of such a commitment. Recognizing the motivations and intentions of my professors sheds additional light on all they offer.

As Kathy and I worked to arrange my student teaching placement I found myself humbled by the amount of time and energy she was willing to invest in finding an appropriate setting for me. Our late-night phone calls, her conversations with others in the department, the sheer number of hours she spent on me (and other students being placed) – all of this powerfully illustrated to me that what she and many others were doing was much more than a job to them. They were investing in me and in the potential they could see within me. Through their actions, my teachers modeled for me a connection between faith, learning, and life that is not necessarily evidenced elsewhere in higher education.

Many times during the past four years I have felt as though I were majoring in "life" and minoring in my particular disciplines. Rather than studying in order to earn a good living, I have learned how to better live out the faithful life I am called to. This under-standing has come as much from observing the lives of those around me as it has from the content of my courses. As I make con-nections between faith, life, and learning for myself, the modeling I see serves to enforce and develop ideas I encounter in classes.

This modeling and living out our faith is a two-way street. While students may be on the receiving end of some of this, they also are on the giving end. Students call me to accountability, to thinking about what is most important, to continually refine what it is in education or methodology that is important. They spur me to action consistent with my words. They are examples of life lived fully. Without interaction, both giving and receiving, I would not have the opportunity to learn and stretch in the same way. One example of our co-learning is the writing of this essay. Scott and I chose to co-author a paper about Mennonite higher education because we were both interested in the topic, we both had done work on the subject in other contexts, and we both consider our-selves Mennonite educators. The idea that I can explore areas of my professional life and faith at a scholarly level with students is a delight and a gift. It is a privilege and treasure to have colleagues of all ages and generations with whom to think – to be able to col-laborate on projects that pertain directly to our lives and how we integrate faith in our professions.

I think it is safe to say that the richness of Goshen College comes much more from the people – the community – than it does from any one aspect of our curriculum. This includes the already addressed aspects of faculty-student interaction at GC – informali-ty, mutual respect, and openness. Part of the informality may come from Mennonite church structures that have avoided clergy-laity distinctions and instead emphasized the brotherhood and sister-hood of all believers. Titles and formal names generally are not used in Mennonite congregations, and neither are they regularly used at Goshen College. Many of my professor-student relation-ships feel more collegial than they do hierarchical. It is clear to me that my professors respect me and this, in turn, invites me to recip-rocate that respect. When this two-way respect is formed, learning begins to feel more dialogical than monological.

In addition to these distinctions in *content* at Goshen College, we also suggested earlier that the *context* of student-faculty social interactions has some unique aspects. One particularly striking aspect is that many students and faculty know each other in multiple contexts. While I interact with students in class, there are also numerous students I see every Sunday morning at church and, at this point, four students I see every Wednesday night as a part of my small group from church. In this context we share different aspects of our lives, talk concretely about how we live out our faith, share our concerns and joys, and deal with the "business" of the church. My husband and I led a Study-Service Term two years ago, and that was another context in which to know and be with students. When we go to the local coffee shop in the evenings we often have a chance to chat with colleagues and students who are there. And frequently my students end up being my colleagues in the public schools when they graduate and become teachers. This ability to know people in many contexts of their lives enhances the educational context as well.

I think there is great value in off-campus interaction with professors. Attending church, working at the Mennonite Relief Sale, or traveling on choir tour with my teachers provides for more informal, less explicitly academic interaction. Back in the classroom after such experiences, we as students can see better just how teaching fits into the lives of our professors. We also better understand that they are "whole people" since we know where they are coming from and how their life experiences contribute to their teaching.

Another context we are aware of is that, because our lives are interwoven and also because this is a residential campus, we often have classroom conversations that move from course to course or that spring from campus-wide issues. Often a discussion in a colleague's course might come up in mine. Last year there was considerable discussion of personal rights and the ethics of freedom. That is as important in education as it is in religion, philosophy, or English literature. My course benefited from the fact that a number of students brought the conversation from an ethics course into mine. This happens not only for Martin Luther King, Jr. Study Day, when our courses focus on particular content relevant to MLK, Jr.'s life, but when other big issues arise on campus – use of campus space, issues in campus housing, current discussions in student government, new requirements in general education, or the latest negotiations between the administration and the cafeteria. All these aspects of life become a part of the informal lunchroom and sidewalk conversation as well as the formal course conversation.

Especially in the later years of my college experience, I have found myself having frequent, informal and meaningful conversations with my friends about pedagogy or about their major areas. As Kathy has mentioned, issues often surface in many different contexts on campus. Talking with other students about how these issues fit into their discipline often sheds new light on how they relate to mine. Also, on many occasions, my friends and I have spent hours discussing Goshen College itself – what this community means to us, its benefits, its shortcomings. These discussions help us to better frame our experiences here and put them into perspective as we prepare to leave this place.

We need to be mindful, though, as this very inter-wovenness can also be our Achilles heel. Many students come to campus knowing or being known by others – students and professors alike. I have a number of students whose parents were colleagues of mine. Many on this campus are related to at least one other person at GC. My brother might have been in a Mennonite Central Committee assignment with someone else's parents. While this can be seen as a rich interweaving of textures – of students "being known" when they come and not slipping through the cracks, it also can easily be confining or, worse yet, exclusive. Indeed, we need to be careful about how these pre-existing relationships shape the experiences of students. While for some there may be a desire to be known, others may not want to be "boxed" by these prior relationships or excluded because of a lack of these connections.

While there can be pre-existing relationships, both positive and negative, my experience has been that faculty often go beyond the "surface level" when relating with students. In many cases, faculty seem to be intentional about identifying strengths and gifts of students in order to foster effective and appropriate use of these aspects of character. A powerful analogy GC's present administrators sometimes use for Mennonite education is that of naming, helping fashion meaning and purpose for students, crafting their contexts and their connections. Experiences I have shared at GC have prompted people (consciously or subconsciously) to name me – to foster in me a clearer and stronger sense of who I am and what I believe, and to name my calling. With this naming I don't feel as though my future has been dictated, but rather that I have been given purpose and perspective which is more than the sum of my academic experiences.

While not every aspect of our campus is as consistent with our faith as we hope it becomes, our sense is that being a Mennonite Church institution can give consistency and focus to all that we do. Our identity can root our educating in our faith if we make the most of the rich context in which we live and work.

---

1. Kathy Meyer Reimer is Associate Professor of Education at Goshen College. Scott Barge, a 1999 GC graduate, is presently Assistant to the Provost at Goshen College.

7

EDUCATION WITH A DIFFERENCE: IMPLEMENTING DREAMS AND REALIZING INTENTIONS

Albert J. Meyer[1]

For over 600 years, from the founding of the first colleges and universities in the Western world, all institutions of higher education were church institutions. Today, fewer than one out of eight students in the United States is attending an institution with any kind of church relationship.[2] Historian Richard Hofstadter has called a "drift toward secularism" the oldest and longest-sustained theme in American higher education.[3]

Is this good? Scientists ordinarily try to report on what *is* without speaking about what is *better* and what is *worse*, but they can, in any case, observe that historians and other commentators have differing points of view and look at what has happened in quite different ways. Some authors and administrators see the contribution of the church to higher education in the past 800 years and say that the church accomplished its mission gloriously – the church led the way, the larger society is now assuming its rightful responsibility, and the church can now turn to new worlds to conquer. Other observers say that the withdrawal of the church from the educational and cultural scene and from a lively engagement with the younger generations in our times is portending greater problems for the societal role and witness of the church in the world of the future.

These observers differ so dramatically because they have different visions for what the church should have been doing or should be doing in higher education in the first place. Differences on missions of schools rooted in different church traditions are often based even more fundamentally on differences in the ecclesiologies of different denominations. In some times and places, churches have started colleges and other institutions with the hope that they would become public institutions as soon as the larger society was ready to assume responsibility for them. The early colleges of the Congregational Church were intended to bring learning to the New World and to help civilize the wilderness. Pioneering in the establishment of institutions needed by the larger society has been an important contribution of the church throughout the centuries. Dissociation and secularization are a part of the church's *intention* for these institutions.

But in other times and places, churches with a countercultural vision founded colleges designed to give a distinctively Christian kind of education that the larger pluralistic society could not appropriately support. When, under the influence of outside societal pressures, those colleges drifted away from the earlier vision of their churches and school leaders, the dissociation was characterized as *unintended* and unfortunate.

Researchers have said for decades that colleges with distinctive missions and clear niches will be more likely to survive and gain strength in the long-term future than will those trying to be all things to all people. For example, one of the most recent reports of a small-college closing said, "Shifting strategies, lack of a niche, and unrealistic projections doomed Bradford .... It tried to weld together a hodgepodge of appeals to different constituencies .... Bradford never clearly articulated who its student body was .... The college did build up special ties, but never comprehensively marketed them ...." A small-college consultant "recommended that Bradford define its specialties, concentrate on them, and get rid of everything else." The college failed to do that.[4]

The problem for those who would like to see at least some markedly *churchly* church colleges and universities is that all too often in the history of American higher education the increasing distance of a college from its sponsoring church was *not* intended by either college *or* church. Richard Hofstadter implied this when he referred to secularization in North American history as a "drift." Indeed, as several major recent studies have emphasized, dissociation frequently has been the long-term and unintended outcome of actions taken in response to immediate challenges by church and school leaders who were deeply committed to having colleges and universities as an ongoing part of the work of the church. Many of those past leaders were denominational executives and church-ordained presidents. Typically, dissociation has not been a part of the conscious intention of either college or church, at least until the distance between church and school has reached a point where the trend is irreversible.

The earliest forebears of today's Mennonites were academics – students of classical and biblical languages at the universities of Paris, Basel, Zurich, and Vienna. Many of these earliest leaders were tortured and martyred. Years of intense persecution led many of their followers to seek peace in places of rural isolation.

In the late 19th and early 20th centuries, American Mennonites re-entered the academic scene as relative newcomers. As such, they now have the opportunity to learn from the longer experiences of those of other traditions. They need not be too critical of those who have gone before; Mennonites can, however, be blamed if they simply repeat the mistakes of their predecessors. The landscape is replete with instances of church-school dissociation. If that is not what they want, Mennonites can learn from these many cases of unintended dissociation. If they hope to go against the stream in establishing and maintaining mutually beneficial relationships, Mennonite churches and higher education institutions need to analyze the factors that will make this possible, and then do what they need to do to realize their intentions.

Mennonites and their schools need to know who they are theologically, but this will not help them have good schools if they do not understand the dynamics of extra-congregational higher educational organizations – that is, how church colleges and universities work.

The challenge for organizational theorists is to explain why organizations change as they do – sometimes in directions very different from those intended by their leaders. The challenge for administrators is to find ways of implementing intentions. Both are important.

General Observations

In view of the dominance of the trend toward church-school dissociation in North American higher education, it is remarkable that, until the past decade, there were almost no studies analyzing the detailed dynamics of this phenomenon. Hundreds of institutional histories describe the evolution of given colleges and universities, dozens of denominational historical studies summarize what has happened, and histories of American higher education record the reality of dissociation, but until recent years there have been almost no serious analytical works on the dissociation process.[5]

The assumption seems to be that the increasing distance between churches and their schools was the product of the changing role of the Western church and a general secularization of certain cultural and intellectual elites in North American society. Certainly these are significant factors. But understanding these factors does not address the question: If dissociation is not what Mennonites (or those in other traditions) want, can they chart a different course? If so, how?

The secularization of certain Western sub-populations is indeed a part of the landscape in which churches live and work today, but in the past, non-supportive or hostile environments have not always meant that churches needed to withdraw from engagement. The dynamics of the increasing distance of churches from their institutions of higher education need further analysis.

Let me begin, then, with several general observations:

1. Dissociation typically occurs over relatively long periods of time.

American college and university presidents serve an average of 6.7 years. The outcomes of steps taken by denominational leaders or a given president are often not evident until many years later. During his or her tenure, a president who is a denominational leader and an outgoing administrator and who relates well personally to the institution's publics will sometimes gain the reputation of maintaining and even enhancing church-school relationships. While important factors may contribute toward long-term dissociation, a charismatic president deeply committed to a church can, with the best of intentions, "warm up" personal relationships with church constituents and make the effects of the fundamental trend factors less visible. There is a remarkable "cut flower" phenomenon – the ethos of a campus can reflect the nourishment of earlier roots for some time after the roots have been cut. It may become evident only years later that the president set in motion certain forces that resulted, over the long-term, in the dissociation of the school from its church roots. By the time the long-term changes are obvious to everyone, it is often too late to reverse the factors making further change inevitable.[6]

2. The dissociation typically involves a gradually increasing vagueness and lack of specificity about the school's mission.

A formerly Presbyterian college will typically, for example, have moved from calling itself "Presbyterian" to calling itself generically "church-related" and "Christian," then "religious," then "historically religious," and finally "value-oriented." Christians interested in schools that are different today will need to talk about authentic Christian commitments as they understand them – not just civic values that were held by state university faculty members almost universally a hundred years ago or by most educated, liberal North Americans today.

Mennonites have some beliefs that are fairly widely understood and accepted in academic circles today – peace, service, environmental stewardship, and so on. But they also have some important and distinctive "values" (if we want to use that rather general term) that are not particularly popular in liberal North American circles just now. If Mennonites and others with distinctive beliefs and practices want to learn from others' experiences, and if they want to pay for having schools in a time when there are plenty of other schools, their colleges will need to be straightforward about their distinctive commitments, not just about values that happen to be popular in conservative or academic circles in the surrounding society today.

3. The unintended long-term "secularization" of schools that have been church-related has frequently been due to actions of church leaders as well as to those of school leaders.

One can, for example, reflect on a 1990 document of the Association of Presbyterian Colleges and Universities, which noted that although "education and the strong support of educational institutions" were among "the historic and theological hallmarks of ... Presbyterianism," this "emphasis is lacking in current statements of mission and mission priority" of leading church bodies. Noting that "involvement in higher education is close to the essence of Presbyterianism," the document continued, "Next to the collective investment of human and financial resources in parish churches ..., the collective investment of people ... and money in ... higher education represents, by far, the largest single domestic enterprise of our denomination .... This makes the lack of attention and concern about higher education [in official circles] all the more surprising." Perhaps prophetically, the statement concluded that "some of the developments we have observed may be irreversible. The Presbyterian Church could be close to a point where its involvement in higher education might be lost forever." In 1993 the Presbyterian Church U.S.A. terminated its Committee on Higher Education, the church body relating to its 68 colleges and universities.

Very few colleges and universities have reversed course after substantial "secularization" – especially after faculty composition and student body mix have reached a certain point. I have observed the unusual case of one Catholic college and a few instances of church high schools that have changed course. The change typically has been difficult and painful.

4. Church-related colleges and universities are subject to legitimacy forces (that is, being seen as schools that can be accepted as such in the conventional use of the term) and pressures toward mimetic isomorphism (that is, toward being "morphed" into the shape of leading schools in their organizational field).

From an organization-theoretical standpoint, "the liberal arts college" and "the research university" are institutions of American society. When churches or other groups of Americans establishing an organization call it a "college," they are buying into a well-established institution of their larger society. Almost all of the answers to questions anyone might have about the college will be assumed, not only by faculty members, but also by prospective students, parents, donors, the local community, government officials, and Americans at large. What a departmental faculty member might be expected to do, what kinds of officers might appear in the administrative cabinet, what the president and board might look like and how they should function, what the school year might be – even the kinds of gowns and hoods faculty members should wear at commencement – all will be taken for granted. If the new organization is called a "college," then everyone will have a fairly clear general impression of what it is going to be; the American college is a well-established and widely understood American institution.[7]

Years ago, sociologist David Riesman referred to American higher education as a "snake-like procession," with Harvard at the head and other colleges and universities following a Harvard model of excellence. To a certain degree, contemporary organizational theorists would confirm this as an accurate description of higher education as it is currently institutionalized in American society. In this situation, non-conformist colleges will need to be very clear with their internal and external constituencies on what they are wanting to do and how they are wanting to do it. Institutional dynamics can far outweigh the good intentions of distinctive schools and churches.

Factors in Lively, Long-Term Church-School Relationships

Looking at the process in more detail, we can ask about the steps through which school and church leaders who want to maintain strong church-school relationships find themselves moving gradually along the well-worn path toward dissociation. What can church and school leaders identify as areas where they will need to effect systemic change if they do not want to move toward dissociation, but rather want to follow a path toward warm and mutually helpful church-school relationships in the future?

Like a family system, an institutionalized organizational system comprises interacting elements. Change in one element can affect the equilibrium of the whole and can lead over time to systemic change. In what follows, I will list four out of a longer list of inter-acting elements in the present institutionalization of higher educa-tion that will need the attention of schools and churches that want to work together in distinctive missions over longer periods of time.

1. Faculty recruitment

Many observers agree that the hiring of faculty members is a key to a church school's fulfillment of its Christian mission. But few have asked how the rhetoric is to be implemented in practice in an aca-demic world. Responsibility for recruitment contacts is increasingly delegated to departments in a culture in which it is gauche and some-times almost illegal to ask personal questions about religion. To achieve hiring goals, creative administrators and faculty members must be able and willing to develop faculty recruitment initiatives considerably different from those currently institutionalized in American academia.[8]

The present faculty recruitment system in American institutions is based on a selection paradigm. A vacancy is announced, candidates apply, some are invited to visit, and a candidate with requisite qualifi-cations is selected and invited. The gifts of promising and entrepre-neurial young people and members of underrepresented groups who have decided not to pursue advanced graduate studies in today's Ph.D. market are lost – they do not even appear on the radar screen. The cul-tivation of candidates who are able to make special contributions to the institution's distinctive mission and the exclusion of candidates who are not really interested in the mission are sometimes left to the decision of a top university administrator who interviews only a few prospects near the end of the process. Such cultivation and exclusion are not integral steps built into the early stages of the search.[9] If under-standing and support for an institution's mission is a significant factor in faculty hiring, it needs to be structured into the whole hiring process in a more integral way.

The mission of the institution and its relevance for hiring need to be clear. If the institution calls itself Christian, for example, does that mean asking only that faculty members refrain from actively oppos-ing the idea of a Christian institution? Would a physics department find it adequate to ask that physics instructors refrain from actively opposing the idea of physics as a discipline? Would it not want to have enough physics instructors who know something about physics and are actual practicing physicists? Should not these physicists show a little enthusiasm for the study of nature?

One of the great obstacles to change in today's recruitment procedures is the idea that "there are lots of good people out there." There are lots of people. But searching within a five-month vacancy window for the combination of theological maturity, teaching ability, and potential for creative work in an academic discipline can pose serious challenges. A multi-dimensional search can start with hundreds of applicants and end up with a null set. There are not lots of Nobel laureates. How many Baptist-interested black women Ph.D. physicists who have a gift for exciting teaching will a Baptist college interested in racial and gender diversity be able to recruit if the outstanding candidates also have invitations from Harvard?[10]

It is important to note that the present institutionalization of faculty recruitment in American academia is as frustrating for young faculty prospects as it is for church colleges and universities trying to assemble good faculty teams. Hundreds of prospects apply for single openings. Many good students decide on other careers where the odds for employment are more promising. The present system for matching institutional needs with the gifts of faculty prospects needs change.

Engaging in serious searches and assembling teams of faculty members committed to institutions' distinctive missions are going to have to take more of the kinds of efforts the Ivy League universities put into getting Nobel laureates (or professional football teams put into getting good quarterbacks and wide receivers), if Christian universities want to move into more significant intellectual and spiritual leadership in the future.[11] Teams of academic and athletic professionals may get hundreds of applicants, but they do not get Nobel Prize winners or star quarterbacks by advertising in professional journals and assuming that top candidates will come running.

In the last century, the professionalization of the faculty by discipline[12] and the long-term impact of prevailing faculty recruitment practices have probably contributed more to the distancing of church colleges from their churches than any other single factor. A church and a college or university that want to swim against the stream in nurturing lively long-term relationships will have to be prepared to initiate a paradigm shift in the faculty recruitment process.

2. Board and staff personnel and leadership

At the heart of any higher educational institution is, after all, a conception of truth. A Christian college is more than chapels or courses in religion or treating students as "whole persons." It has to be built on an understanding of what is true. To the degree that a church and its schools have distinctive conceptions of what is true and important, it is reasonable to anticipate that they will have curricula and extra-curricula based on these understandings.[13]

The other essays in this volume focus on curricula and extra-curricula – the experiences students encounter as they move from entrance to graduation. Apart from what students do in educating each other in college settings, most student change and development is a product of what faculty members teach in their classrooms, share in their offices, provide in off-campus experiences, and model in their lives. Much of what faculty members actually teach and share is influenced by their disciplinary associations, but as we have seen, schools that are concerned about the development of their students in non-cognitive areas of growth need administrators and faculty members also committed to this mission.

But who ultimately identifies the long-term mission? Who is ultimately responsible for the choice of the president and chief administrative officers? Many observers of the past decade have commented on the weakness of typical American non-profit trustees in clearly identifying the long-term missions of the institutions they are supposed to hold in trust and implementing procedures that will enable their institutions to fulfill their missions. Several foundations have tried to effect change in this area by supporting projects on trustee boards.

Pressures on educational administrators for short-term results are enormous. Short-term institutional pressures and interests can come into sharp conflict with long-term church goals. A college administrator may, for example, be expected to get more contributed dollars. Sometimes the faculty loses its confidence in the president if the president does not bring in the dollars; the president's own survival is sometimes at stake. To help broaden the college's appeal, the administrator urges the addition of wealthy non-church constituents to the board of trustees. This has little impact on church relationships initially, since the large board and sponsoring church typically look to the president for the academic and spiritual leadership of the college. The impact comes, however, when the church wakes up, sometimes at the selection of a new president, to discover that the board is not adequately concerned about the churchly mission of the institution, and that the board with the non-committed members now carries major responsibilities in the selection of the new president as well as important legal responsibilities for the future of the institution.

In the system of which Goshen College is a part, there has been a church-wide board that has come to see its primary task as that of taking actions and setting policies that implement the long-term mission of its schools.[14] Effective dual-board arrangements are unusual among church schools; they are very common in the public sector as ways of providing for relationships between a society and its institutions.

In any case, boards have special responsibilities for representing long-term institutional interests. A church without appropriate ways of assuring long-term as well as short-term interests in its relationship to its colleges and universities will almost inevitably find itself at increasing distance from its schools.

3. Student peer environment

A college or university must have a board and faculty members committed to a distinctive mission if it is to implement its goals. Having students committed to the mission is not always as critical, but a church and a school need to be aware of how the student peer environment can affect the school's fulfillment of its mission.

The studies of Theodore Newcomb and others on the impact of colleges on students[15] first highlighted the importance of an institution's student culture for the growth and development of its students. In some areas, including those of most interest to the church, the impact of students on their peers is significantly greater than the impact of faculty members on their students. Indeed, in some of these areas one can say that the principal faculty-administration influence is in providing for arrangements that attract to the campus the kind of students needed to achieve the institution's mission. From that point on, the chain reaction among the students themselves takes over and is most effective in producing the desired student outcomes.

Educating students at large is certainly a contribution to the larger society. Churches have made urgently needed contributions in schools in the developing world for students not initially interested in church perspectives. Whether educating students at large should be a church priority in a society that is already assuming its responsibility for sponsoring many other good schools is a matter for church discernment. Historically, a decline in the proportion of interested students in a school has sometimes contributed to a lowered church interest in and support of the school. Whether a church's effectiveness over the long run in its mission to interested students is attenuated by the presence of many students attending only for reasons of proximity, convenience, or academic program needs to be considered.

In this area again, short-term interests and pressures can get in the way if a church cannot assure that long-term considerations are given priority. For example, a church college or university administrator wants a higher enrollment. To get more students, the administrator appeals to students whether or not they have any particular interest in the institution's mission. In the past decade, "enrollment management" was approached with greater intentionality than in earlier years, but often the focus was more on numbers and academic criteria than on "fit." A school with a church mission needs to be concerned about applicants' potential ability to profit from and contribute to the aspects of the campus culture of special importance for the institution's mission.

4. A church with a distinctive mission

In their classic work on American higher education, Christopher Jencks and David Riesman of Harvard spoke of the future of Protestant colleges in these words:

> The future of recognizably Protestant colleges ...
> seems to depend on the survival within the larger
> society of Protestant enclaves whose members
> believe passionately in a way of life radically different from that of the majority, and who are both
> willing and able to pay for a brand of higher education that embodies their vision.[16]

Church schools with distinctive missions depend not only on board goals, faculty commitments, and interested students, but also on churches committed to the schools' distinctive missions in the larger environment. A church must say – in its structures, as well as in its financial contributions and denominational statements – that the academic preparation of tomorrow's generation is an important part of the mission and work of today's church.

As I have noted, a typical dissociation pattern evolved where denominations delegated responsibility for their higher educational institutions to institutional presidents. The denominations typically felt that the professional staffs of their colleges and universities could recruit students and raise funds better than their denominational staffs, so they left their institutions to their own devices. As denominational leaders became less interested, the institutions became increasingly independent. Or, to put it in other terms, their church relationships became less important, and they became more dependent on other sources for faculty members, students, dollars, and legitimation.

Beyond the abandonment of their institutional leaders, denominational leaders frequently evaluated the work of their institutional presidents and administrations in terms of short-term criteria not necessarily correlated with the long-term accomplishment of the schools' religious missions – in terms of criteria such as growth in numbers, buildings, and net worth.

It takes a strong church to have strong church schools. But good church schools can play a vital role in helping a church stay on the cutting edge in the churchly mission in which both have significant parts and a long-term interest.

The Future

The future need not be determined by the past. We can best plan for the future, however, if we begin by facing realistically the available information on recent experience and current trends. We have to face realistically, for example, the fact that Goshen College is the only Mennonite college on the top Carnegie list of "national four-year liberal arts colleges in the United States," and that, of the 162 colleges in this Carnegie category, there is a negative correlation between reputational excellence and any kind of self-reported church relationship. We have to face the fact that Mennonites have some beliefs and practices that are not reflected in ratings of reputational excellence. And we have to face the fact that, as we have seen, the current trend continues to be toward greater church-school distance and dissociation.

A school cannot be a church-related school over the long term if the church is not ready to give it the moral and tangible support it needs for its part in the church's mission. On the other hand, a church will not, over the long term, give substantial churchly support to a school hardly different from other independent and public schools in its purposes and programs.

There are, then, challenges for innovative church and school administrators. More research is needed; good dissertation projects abound for young researchers interested in working on some cutting-edge questions. Churches and schools are not likely to make necessary systemic changes if they believe that the future should be an attempt to continue the past. Patterns that seemed adequate among most church colleges in the recent past in such areas as faculty recruitment, board functioning, enrollment management, and church relationship are inadequate for maintaining mutually health-giving relationships and distinctive school niches in the future.

Earlier chapters in this text referred to Goshen College's Study-Service Term (SST). Over 30 years ago Goshen College pioneered in making the study term, usually in the developing world, a part of the general education program for all students. It grew out of a Committee on the Future of the College formed by President Paul Mininger and staffed by Henry Weaver, who provided remarkable leadership in bringing the faculty to a decision that was essentially unanimous on the idea. Weaver was an administrator who had unusual gifts for getting foundation or government support, but he and his colleagues were unable to find any significant outside grants for initiating SST. Educators of that time saw the Study-Service Term as marginal, a funny idea, "not real education" – perhaps like requiring students to have a semester of playing chess. And the conventional wisdom of articulate top experts in international education in those times was that only a few carefully selected North American college students could have good learning experiences in developing parts of the world. Goshen College went ahead anyhow.

The rest is history. The world has changed. Now everyone is talking about global education. In recent weeks, the Clinton Administration identified as a policy priority increasing the number of American students studying abroad and getting more colleges and universities to offer study-abroad programs.[17] Goshen had a good idea. It was just ahead of its time.

North Americans are facing major domestic and international challenges as they look to the future. The question for our Mennonite college presidents, their administrative colleagues and boards, their faculties, Mennonite churches, and other supporters of Mennonite higher education is: On the basis of their religious heritage and vision, what can and should Goshen and other Mennonite colleges be doing now that others may consider crazy but that will be seen as innovative 30 years from now? Mennonites have the possibility of engaging in academic pioneering as an important part of their mission in today's world.

---

1. Albert J. Meyer was Executive Secretary and President of the Mennonite Board of Education from 1967 to 1995, and continues to serve the organization as Senior Research Associate. The author expresses appreciation to Bethel College (Kansas), where he was invited to deliver the 1993 Menno Simons Lectures on "The Church and Higher Education"; to Princeton University, which hosted him as visiting fellow for 13 months in 1995-1996; and to the Mennonite Board of Education, which has encouraged his reflection and study in this area since 1966. The present text is adapted from a paper presented at a Rhodes Consultation on the Future of the Church-Related College conference on The Church-Related College's Postmodern Opportunity, 2-4 May 1997, under the title, "Factors in Churches' Formation and Maintenance of Value-Distinctive Higher Educational Institutions: An Open Systems Inquiry." The primary database for the present work has been personal consultation and study visits to over 80 institutions in the United States and Canada over the years; 32 case studies in two foundation-supported projects; and work at and visits over the years to over 35 colleges, universities, and theological faculties in Europe, Africa, and Asia.

2. Information from a special database of church-affiliated colleges and universities prepared by Donald Garber of the Mennonite Board of Education from information from the National Center for Educational Statistics, contacts with denominational offices, and, in some instances, reports from institutions.

3. Richard Hofstadter, "The Age of the College," in Richard Hofstadter and C. DeWitt Hardy, eds., *The Development and Scope of Higher Education in the United States* (New York: Columbia University Press, 1952), 3.

4. Martin van der Werf, "The Death of a Small College," *The Chronicle of Higher Education* 46:36 (12 May 2000), A40. In North Central Association assignments, I have visited two other church-related institutions that have closed in the past three years.

5. From an organization-theoretical perspective, one of the reasons there have been so few analyses of the available data is that no one has had this role in existing institutions. As Manning Pattillo and Don Mackenzie reported in their Danforth Commission report already in the 1960s (*Church-Sponsored Higher Education in the United States* [Washington, D.C.: American Council on Education, 1966], 276-277), most church bodies have not had strong denominational agencies and offices expected to be asking long-term questions about their involvements in higher education. In their preliminary report in 1965, they called this a source of "major weakness of church-affiliated higher education." Pattillo and Mackenzie reported that churches have typically asked their institutional presidents to represent their church interests in higher education. These presidents have typically served for relatively short terms and have needed to cope with short-term challenges. The institutional leaders have typically not been in a position to say, for example, that their institutions should make sacrifices in a three-to-five-year time frame in order to better fulfill their missions in a 30-to-50-year frame of reference. If they wanted to be "successful" leaders, they were expected by church and school people alike to meet shorter-term goals that then led in the long run toward dissociation.

6. Case: The University of Notre Dame, a flagship Roman Catholic research university, certainly has a distinctive campus ethos today. Most students are Catholic. There is a crucifix in every classroom. The predecessor to its current president served with distinction for 35 years as a denominational and educational leader – he had a deep commitment to the church relationship of his university. But, in putting the university on the map with other leading research universities, he brought increasing numbers of faculty members to the campus largely on the basis of their academic qualifications. The percentage of self-identified Catholics has fallen in recent decades – it fell from 64 to 56 percent just in the past decade. In this most recent decade, in spite of canon law, papal statements, bishops' papers, and university policy on faculty composition, Catholics comprised only 45 percent of the university's new regular faculty hires. It has been said that some of the new non-Catholic faculty members are deeply committed to the Catholic character of the institution – and this is certainly true in individual instances. A careful study, however, shows that: 1) many Catholic faculty members are not particularly committed to the Catholic mission of the university; and 2) that the non-Catholic faculty members are, overall, less committed to the Catholic character of the school. If the percentage of non-Catholic faculty hires would continue to increase as rapidly as it did in recent decades, the ethos will change over time. Indeed, some changes are already evident. Less than five years after the arrival of the current president, the university's faculty senate introduced a no-confidence resolution over the role of the faculty in university governance. The big faculty issue several years ago was the president's appointment of a member of the university's sponsoring religious order to the faculty, over the rejection of the candidate by the department involved. The faculty is not at all agreed on its role vis-a-vis that of the church. A generalization from past experience would indicate that a university cannot long maintain a distinctive mission without adequate support in the faculty for that mission. Changes initiated decades ago are

having effects that are hardly visible in the campus ethos and public mind today. It may be several decades and several presidents from now before changes that may already be irreversible are fully visible.

7. In addition to the local and global institutional forces discussed here, it should be noted that typical colleges and universities have all kinds of linkages with outside associations and agencies. Government-sponsored schools are accountable to and sustained by their mandating societies. In a recent publication, James Burtchaell comments on the "dogma of 'institutional autonomy.'" In two full pages of rather playful musing, he lists over 50 specific linkages of a typical "independent" college or university with outside associations and agencies. Some of these involve formal accountability. Burtchaell concludes: "No university is an asteroid. It is an organic member of a complex, very endocrine community." See "Out of the Heartburn of the Church," *The Journal of College and University Law* 25:4 (1999), 656-695.

8. The aging of faculty and uncapping of retirement are making faculty recruitment particularly critical. See Robert L. Clark and Brett Hammond, "As Professors Age, Retirement Policies Need Rejuvenation: Few Administrators Grasp the Implications of the Impending Changes in Faculty Age Structures and Retirement Patterns," *The Chronicle of Higher Education* (2 June 2000), B7ff.

9. Just this past year I became aware of another instance in which a president turned down one candidate and then, three months later, thinking he had used up his "capital" for the time, reluctantly felt he could not turn down an unqualified candidate in another department without inciting an insurrection. An observer does not need advanced study in organizational theory to see that a system in which important criteria are introduced by a single officer late in the recruitment process – or the present Roman Catholic requirement that a bishop without adequate time allocation, a special staff, or agreed-upon procedures is supposed to ascertain the theological faithfulness of Catholic instructors in theology in colleges and universities in his diocese – will inevitably lead to unnecessary impasses and conflicts and cannot serve as effective ways of working in the long run.

10. I am aware of several instances of the recruitment of highly gifted prospects of underrepresented populations in which the prospects chose even relatively small church colleges when they actually had invitations from Harvard or Princeton. The colleges' strong church relationships were positive, not negative, factors – indeed, they were the deciding factors. But these unusual instances of the successful recruitment of outstanding but unlikely prospects have typically been the product of years of search and courting, not of assuming good candidates would suddenly appear in response to advertisements in *The Chronicle of Higher Education.*

11. Studies in Princeton's recent anniversary year pointed again to the role of Dean Henry Burchard Fine's work in faculty recruitment (supported by his presidents) in transforming the small colonial College of New Jersey of the 1800s into the major research university Princeton is in this century. In his earlier chapter in this volume, Theron Schlabach highlights the importance for Goshen College in the past century of President Sanford Yoder's hiring of Noah Oyer, Harold Bender, and other remarkably gifted leaders, even at some risk, for his new faculty in 1924. In the past year or two, *The Chronicle of Higher Education* and the daily press have increasingly reported on strategies for longer-term departmental development in major universities and the "hot pursuit" of leading scholars.

12. This is the "Academic Revolution" referred to by Christopher Jencks and David Riesman in their classic work of that title (Garden City: Doubleday, 1968). It has brought many benefits. We have stronger disciplinary associations, and they have contributed to American higher education's strength. The point here, however, is that competence in research in a discipline is not the sole criterion for contribution as a classroom teacher in a school with a special mission.

13. See Parker Palmer, *Christian Century* (21 October 1981), 1051ff.; Parker Palmer, *To Know As We Are Known* (San Francisco: Harper & Row, Publishers, 1983); and Douglas Sloan, *Faith and Knowledge: Mainline Protestantism and American Higher Education* (Louisville: Westminster John Knox Press, 1994).

14. Brief descriptions of the arrangement can be found in Robert Rue Parsonage, ed., *Church Related Higher Education: Perceptions and Perspectives* (Valley Forge: Judson Press, 1978), 222-223; and Victor Stoltzfus, *Church-Affiliated Higher Education: Exploratory Case Studies* (Goshen: Pinchpenny Press, 1992), 118-121. A more recent description would place even more emphasis on the role of the church-wide board in fulfilling long-term goals and intentions in an environment in which institutional administrators and boards are subject to enormous short-term pressures. The church-wide board needs somewhat greater distance from day-to-day operations. The system requires those concerned with short-term needs; it also requires those who are responsible for the implementation of long-term objectives.

15. Theodore M. Newcomb and Everett K. Wilson, *College Peer Groups: Problems and Prospects for Research,* in the National Opinion Research Center Monographs in Social Research Series (Chicago: Aldine Publishing Company, 1966) and Theodore M. Newcomb et. al., *Persistence and Change: Bennington College and Its Students After Twenty-Five Years* (New York: John Wiley & Sons, 1967). In 1969, Theodore Newcomb, the father of social-psychological researches on the changes colleges produce in students, joined with a younger colleague, Kenneth Feldman, in surveying all research studies of the previous 40 years in a two-volume classic in educational literature, *The Impact of College on Students* (San Francisco: Jossey-Bass). In the next decade, Alexander Astin summarized his own research findings in these words: "Perhaps the most compelling generalization ... is the pervasive effect of the peer group on the individual student's development ....." See his *Four Critical Years: Effects of College on Beliefs, Attitudes, and Knowledge* (San Francisco: Jossey-Bass, 1977), 363.

16. Christopher Jencks and David Riesman, *The Academic Revolution* (Chicago: University of Chicago Press, 1968), 330.

17. Joel Hardi, "Clinton Calls on Federal Agencies to Help Colleges Encourage Foreign Study," *The Chronicle of Higher Education* 46:34 (28 April 2000). Hardi notes that only "about 9 percent of U.S. undergraduates study abroad, ...but less than a third of those spend at least a semester in a foreign country ...." He quotes Secretary of Education Richard Riley as saying, "Surely we can find new ways to encourage many other colleges and universities to become more active in the international arena."

SELECT BIBLIOGRAPHY ON
MENNONITE HIGHER EDUCATION

Augsburger, Myron S. "Christian Realism in Higher Education." Pamphlet of 75th Anniversary Convocation Address at Eastern Mennonite College and Seminary, 3 October 1992.

Beechy, Atlee. "Goshen College and the Teaching of Values: A Report of the Office of Experimentation." Mimeographed paper, June 1970, available in the Mennonite Historical Library (hereafter MHL).

Bender, Philip D. "Mennonite Conceptions of Education, 1894-1923, and the Closing of Goshen College." Unpublished history seminar paper, Goshen College, 1970, available in MHL.

Biesecker-Mast, Gerald J. "The Radical Mission of Teaching and Thinking: The Anabaptist Difference in Mennonite Higher Education," *The Mennonite* (February 1999), 4-6.

Blosser, Don. *The Word Among Us: Teaching the Bible from the Pulpit and in the Classroom*. Goshen: Pinchpenny Press, 1996.

Bush, Perry. *Dancing with the Kobzar: Bluffton College and Mennonite Higher Education, 1899-1999.* Telford: Pandora Press, 2000.

Coffman, John S. *The Spirit of Progress: A Lecture, Delivered at the Opening of the First School Building of the "Elkhart Institute," Elkhart, Ind., Feb. 11, 1896*. Booklet available in MHL.

Epp, Frank H. *Small College Set on a Hill: Reflections on Church College Education in the University Context*. Mimeographed at Conrad Grebel College, University of Waterloo, June 1979.

Fisher Miller, Susan. *Culture for Service: A History of Goshen College, 1894-1994*. Goshen: Goshen College, 1994.

Friesen, Lauren, ed. *Our Learning Environment: Proceedings of the Faculty Workshop, 24-28 August 1987*. Goshen: Goshen College, 1988.

Graber Miller, Keith. "A One-Armed Embrace of Postmodernity: International Education and Church-Related Colleges," in Stephen Haynes and Corrie Norman, eds. *Talking Out of Place: Professing in the Postmodern Academy*. Waco: Baylor University Press, forthcoming.

_____, and Shirley Hershey Showalter, "On Keeping the Faith: Integrity with Your Heritage," in Gary DeKrey, DeAne Lagerquist, and Pamela Schwandt, eds. *Called to Serve: The Vocation of a Church College*. Northfield: St. Olaf, 1999.

Hartzler, John E. *Education Among the Mennonites of America*. Danvers: Central Mennonite Publishing Board, 1925.

Hawkley, Ken, ed. *Mennonite Higher Education: Experience and Vision: A Symposium on Mennonite Higher Education*. Bluffton: Bluffton College, 1992.

Hertzler, Daniel. *Mennonite Education: Why and How? A Philosophy of Education for the Mennonite Church*. Scottdale: Herald Press, 1971.

Huebner, Harry, ed. *Mennonite Education in a Post-Christian World*. Winnipeg: CMBC Publications, 1998.

Hughes, Richard T., and William B. Adrian, eds. *Models for Christian Higher Education: Strategies for Success in the Twenty-First Century*. Grand Rapids: William B. Eerdmans, 1997.

Juhnke, James C. *Dialogue with a Heritage: Cornelius H. Wedel and the Beginnings of Bethel College*. North Newton: Bethel College, 1987.

Kauffmann, Norman L. "The Impact of Study Abroad on Personality Change." Ed.D. dissertation, Indiana University, 1983.

_____, Judith N. Martin, and Henry D. Weaver, with Judy Weaver. *Students Abroad: Strangers at Home: Education for a Global Society*. Yarmouth: Intercultural Press, 1992.

Keim, Paul A., and Keith Graber Miller. "Choice and Fate: Goshen College and Mennonite Identity in the 21st Century," unpublished Goshen College convocation address, 26 February 1999, available from the authors.

Kraybill, Donald B. *Mennonite Education: Issues, Facts and Changes*. Scottdale: Herald Press, 1978.

Lederach, Paul. "The Mission of Our Church Related Colleges," Parts I and II. Unpublished presentations, Mennonite Board of Education and College Boards Meeting, Phoenix, Arizona, 14 November 1997, available from the author.

Martin, John D. *Christopher Dock: Pioneer Christian Schoolmaster on the Skippack*. Harrisonburg: Christian Light, 1971.

Meyer, Albert J. "The Church and Higher Education." Unpublished Menno Simons Lectures at Bethel College, North Newton, Kansas, October-November 1993, available in MHL.

_____. "Needed: A Mennonite Philosophy of Higher Education," *Mennonite Life* 17:1 (January 1962), 3-4.

Miller, Mary. *A Pillar of Cloud: The Story of Hesston College*, 1909-1959. North Newton: Mennonite Press, 1959.

Pellman, Hubert R. *Eastern Mennonite College, 1917-1957: A History.* Harrisonburg: Eastern Mennonite College, 1967.

Showalter, Shirley Hershey. "An Anabaptist-Mennonite Model for Christian Higher Education." Unpublished paper presented at Abilene Christian University, 27 February 1998, available from the author.

_____. "How Does a Mennonite Model Work in Actual Practice? The Case of Goshen College." Unpublished paper presented at the Models for Christian Higher Education: Strategies for Success in the 21st Century conference, University of Notre Dame, 12 June 1998, available from the author.

_____. "Integrating Anabaptist/Christian Faith and Values into the Programs of Mennonite Colleges." Unpublished paper presented at The Church and College in Partnership: A Vision for the Future, Goshen College, 23-26 March 1995, available from the author.

_____. "A Tale of Three Rivers: Diversity and Spirituality at Goshen College," in Peter Laurence, ed. *Pluralism in the Academy: Education as Transformation*. Wellesley: Wellesley College, forthcoming.

Showalter, Stuart, ed. *The Role of Service-Learning in International Education: Proceedings of a Wingspread Conference, held April 26-28, 1989, at Racine, Wisconsin*. Goshen: Goshen College, 1989.

Stoltzfus, Victor. *Church-Affiliated Higher Education: Exploratory Case Studies of Presbyterian, Roman Catholic and Wesleyan Colleges*. Goshen: Pinchpenny Press, 1992.

Studer, Gerald C. *Christopher Dock, Colonial Schoolmaster: The Biography and Writings of Christopher Dock.* Scottdale: Herald Press, 1993.

Toews, John E. "The Church and Education in the Post-Modern Age." Photocopied presentation, undated, available in MHL.

Toews, Paul, ed. *Mennonite Idealism and Higher Education: The Story of the Fresno Pacific College Idea.* Fresno: The Center for Mennonite Brethren Studies, 1995.

Umble, John S. *Goshen College, 1894-1954: A Venture in Christian Higher Education.* Goshen: Goshen College, 1955.

Wiese, Michael D. "Mennonite Church and Higher Education: Gideon Project, Phases I and II, Final Reports." Unpublished reports, 1996, available from Goshen College Director of Admissions and Enrollment.

Yoder, Paton. "Toward a Mennonite Philosophy of Education Since 1890." Multilithed "Philosophy of Christian Education Study for the Mennonite Church: Workshop Paper C," Hesston, Kansas, 13-16 September 1968, available in MHL.

CONTRIBUTORS

SCOTT BARGE, a 1999 Goshen College graduate in Elementary Education and Teaching English as a Second Language (TESOL), is presently Assistant to the Provost at GC. He has experienced practica in conflict mediation and TESOL and was a student teacher in Elkhart, Goshen, and Penn-Harris-Madison elementary schools. In addition, he spent two summers at Lithuania Christian College in Klaipeda, Lithuania, studying Lithuanian as well as teaching English and writing. While at Goshen and Hesston colleges, Barge received several academic scholarships. Beyond Mennonite higher education, his interests include music, conflict mediation, religion and theology, and travel.

WILBUR J. BIRKY, Director of International Education at Goshen College, received his Ph.D. in English at the University of Iowa. Prior to his present assignment at GC, he taught English at Goshen College from 1964 to 1967 and from 1970 to 1994, and led six Study-Service Term units in Costa Rica and one in China. He spent portions of four other academic years in Asia as director of a summer institute at Northeast University of Technology, Shenyang, China; Visiting Professor in American Literature at Sichuan Foreign Languages University, Chongqing, China; and Visiting Professor at Hokusei University, Sapporo, Japan. In recent years, Birky has spoken extensively on international education at workshops and academic conferences. He also has been Visiting Scholar at the University of Virginia, Lilly Faculty Open Fellow for study in Japan and England, and a Teaching-Research Fellow at the University of Iowa. He has written a number of reviews for academic publications and was co-editor of Contemporary Costa Rican Literature in Translation.

KEITH GRABER MILLER, Professor of Bible, Religion, and Philosophy at Goshen College, received his Ph.D. in Religion from Emory University in 1994. In addition to teaching courses in ethics, theology, religious history, sociology of religion and human sexuality, he has co-led, with his wife Ann, four Study-Service Term units in Dominican Republic. He also has taught several courses at Associated Mennonite Biblical Seminary in the areas of ethics and sexuality. Graber Miller is the author of *Wise as Serpents, Innocent as Doves: American Mennonites Engage Washington*, and has published numerous articles in academic journals and chapters in edited texts, including two other collaborative volumes addressing church-related higher education. He is a member of the Board of Editors of *The Mennonite Quarter Review*, and since 1995 he has been a participant in or associate director of the Rhodes Consultation on the Future of the Church-Related College.

PAUL A. KEIM, Vice President for Academic Affairs and Academic Dean at Goshen College, received his Ph.D. in Near Eastern Languages and Civilizations from Harvard University. Proficient in reading, writing, or speaking 20 ancient and modern languages, Keim continues to teach language courses in addition to his work as Academic Dean. He has studied in Jordan, Poland, and Switzerland, and has taught college or seminary courses in language or religion at Harvard Divinity School, Hesston College, College of Charleston, and Indiana University. From 1980 to 1982 he served with Mennonite Central Committee as country representative in Poland. His writings have been published in a number of academic journals and texts, and he presently is working on several longer works, including a revision of his dissertation, titled "When Sanctions Fail: The Social Function of Curse in Ancient Israel."

ALBERT J. MEYER has analyzed and written about Mennonite higher education more than any other person within the Anabaptist-Mennonite tradition. From 1967 to 1995 he was Executive Secretary and President of the Mennonite Board of Education, and he continues to serve the organization as Senior Research Associate. Meyer has taught or worked as a visiting researcher at Goshen College, New College Berkeley, University of Paris, Bethel College, University of Basel, and Princeton University. He received his Ph.D.

in Physics at Princeton University, and also studied or audited courses in his undergraduate and graduate work in religion, philosophy, and church history. He has spoken extensively at academic conferences on Mennonite higher education, and has published on topics as diverse as "Toward an Anabaptist Theology of Institutions" and "A Double-Source Double-Crystal X-ray Spectrometer for High-Sensitivity Lattice-Parameter Difference Measurements." From November 1995 to December 1996, Meyer was Visiting Fellow at the Center for the Study of American Religion, Princeton University. He continues to serve as a consultant for Mennonite educational institutions and for larger higher-education projects.

KATHY MEYER REIMER received her Ph.D. in Curriculum and Instruction from the University of Illinois in 1991. A 1983 Goshen College graduate, she returned to GC in 1991 in the Education Department, specializing in children's literature, developmental reading, curriculum studies, and reading problems. Prior to completing her master's and doctoral work, she taught first grade and English as a Second Language in Goshen and Elkhart elementary schools. For seven years she co-edited a journal for the National Council of Teachers of English, and she presently serves on the manuscript review boards for two academic journals. Meyer Reimer presents papers regularly at education conferences, and has published articles in several journals and texts. She also has served as a consultant for many local, regional, and national school organizations or school corporations. She and her husband, Paul, co-led a Study-Service Term unit in Dominican Republic in 1997.

THERON F. SCHLABACH, Professor of History at Goshen College, is active in research and writing and occasional teaching. He received his Ph.D. in U.S. Social History from the University of Wisconsin. For nearly 20 years he was a member of the Board of Editors for *The Mennonite Quarterly Review* and from 1992 to 1994 was its Interim and Managing Editor. For many years he has been Editor-in-Chief of Studies in Anabaptist and Mennonite History, an ongoing book series; also, he was Editor of the four Mennonite Experience in America history books and author of one of them, *Peace, Faith, Nation: Mennonites and Amish in Nineteenth-Century America.* He is also author of *Pensions for Professors* (on the origins of the Teachers Insurance and Annuities Association); *Edwin E. Witter: Cautious Reformer* (biography of a key shaper of the U.S. Social Security system); and *Gospel Versus Gospel: Mission and the Mennonite Church, 1863-1944.* And he was co-editor of *Proclaim Peace: Christian Pacifism from Unexpected Quarters.* In addition, he has published various pieces in historical journals and is now writing a life-and-thought biography of Mennonite ethicist Guy F. Hershberger (1896-1989). He has been a Danforth Fellow, National Endowment for the Humanities Research Fellow, Visiting Fellow at University of Notre Dame, and Senior Fellow in Residence at the Young Center for the Study of Anabaptist and Pietist Groups. For Goshen College he led seven Study-Service Term units in Costa Rica.

SHIRLEY HERSHEY SHOWALTER, President of Goshen College, has served in many roles at GC since 1974. Prior to her inauguration as president in 1997, she had been Professor of English, project director for several major institutional grants, Director of Continuing Education, and co-leader of the first Study-Service Term in Côte d'Ivoire, West Africa. While on sabbatical in 1986-87 she was a Faculty Research Associate and Interim Vice President for the Consortium for the Advancement of Private Higher Education in Washington, D.C. In recent years, she has spoken at many academic conferences about Mennonite higher education, with related publications in several academic journals and texts. Showalter, who received her Ph.D. in American Civilization at University of Texas at Austin, also has served as a consultant for Baptist, Catholic and Mennonite organizations and as a formal mentor to a number of postdoctoral fellows and Goshen College students. She presently is a Gallup Fellow, Director of the Council of Independent Colleges, and a board member at the Lantz Center for Christian Vocations, University of Indianapolis.

.